Protection of Civilians in Modern Conflicts and International Humanitarian Law

Protection of Civilians in Modern Conflicts and International Humanitarian Law

Edited by

Pradeep Goswami, AK Bardalai and Kompal Zinta

(Established 1870)

United Service Institution of India

New Delhi (India)

Vij Books
New Delhi (India)

Published by

Vij Books
(Publishers, Distributors & Importers)
4836/24, Ansari Road
Delhi – 110 002
Phones: 91-11-43596460
Mob: 98110 94883
e-mail: contact@vijpublishing.com
web : www.vijbooks.in

First Published in India in 2024

ISBN: 978-81-19438-15-0

Contents

Concept Note

Protection of Civilians in Modern Conflicts and International Humanitarian Law

Introduction

The world is currently facing unprecedented humanitarian crises due to vicious conflicts and environmental catastrophes. The challenges have been further aggravated due to polarisation in the United Nations Security Council and the lack of safeguards to respect International Humanitarian Law (IHL). Ongoing conflicts in various regions, including Africa, Ukraine, and Gaza have highlighted disturbing trends such as the bombing of schools and hospitals, sexual exploitation, and large-scale forced displacement. Such actions violate the norms and laws of war and have a disproportionate impact on innocent civilians, especially those who are internally displaced, disabled, impoverished and constantly face life-and-death situations.

International Humanitarian Law

IHL, also known as the Law of Armed Conflict, regulates the behaviour of parties in armed conflicts by limiting the effects of a conflict and protect those not or no longer taking part in the hostilities[1], such as civilians and wounded or captured combatants. It is primarily embodied in the Geneva Conventions and their Additional Protocols and reflected in customary international law. Even so, the devastating humanitarian consequences of contemporary warfare raise serious questions regarding how parties to such conflicts interpret and apply relevant IHL rules, to balance military necessity and humanity, including the principles of distinction, proportionality, and precautions.

Opinions on interpreting IHL in modern conflicts vary due to the complexity of conflicts involving state and non-state actors, including Private Military Contractors.[2] In contemporary armed conflicts, the line between combatants and civilians is often blurred, especially in urban settings, leading to a significant potential for civilian harm. Ensuring universal respect and compliance with IHL rules[3] is crucial to minimising human suffering in conflict situations.

Protection of Civilians (PoC)

Addressing PoC in modern conflicts requires a comprehensive approach that can respond to the imperative to balance the exigencies of military necessity and the principle of humanity to safeguard civilians who do not participate in hostilities. This includes not only the interpretation and application of IHL but also ensuring accountability for violations of IHL. Enhancing community resilience and supporting post-conflict local peacebuilding efforts are also crucial for mitigating the impact of conflict on civilians.

Purpose

This discussion seeks to address the evolving challenges[4] of contemporary conflicts and explore innovative strategies to enhance the protection of civilians and uphold the principles of IHL, in two sessions as under:

Session I - PoC and Modern Conflicts

- Trends in modern conflicts.

- Challenges to the protection of civilians in armed conflicts.

- IHL and Challenges of modern armed conflict.

Session II - Responding to Challenges of Modern Conflicts

- Challenges of Misinformation, Disinformation, Mal-information and Hate Speech – impact on PoC and Peacekeepers.

- Challenges in the application of IHL and leveraging modern technology to protect civilians.

- Adherence to IHL by state and non-state actors.

Conclusion

This discussion will provide an opportunity to experts, policymakers, and practitioners to exchange insights, share best practices, and identify innovative solutions to the complex challenges of modern conflicts. By fostering dialogue and collaboration, stakeholders aim to contribute to a more secure and peaceful world, where the principles of PoC and IHL are upheld and respected.

Welcome Remarks

Major General PK Goswami, VSM (Retd)
Deputy Director General and Head UN Centre, USI

The United Service Institution of India (USI) has made consistent efforts to highlight the predicament of civilians, consequent to armed conflicts through seminars and conferences on United Nations Peacekeeping and International Humanitarian Law (IHL). During 2023, the USI organised a seminar on IHL and Peacekeeping on 21 and 22 Nov 2023. In continuation of these efforts, this seminar on 'Protection of Civilians in Modern Conflicts and International Humanitarian Law', was jointly organised by the USI and the International Committee of the Red Cross (ICRC). It focuses on protecting civilians in modern conflicts and responding to the challenges of contemporary conflicts.

The world has changed drastically in the last 25 years since the United Nations Security Council (UNSC) first established the Protection of Civilians (PoC) as a crucial international peace and security issue with Resolution 1265 (1999). In the prevailing geopolitical churning and shifting alliances, the world is witnessing growing geopolitical tensions and a manifold increase in armed conflicts, triggering humanitarian crises. Armed conflicts have become increasingly complex, urbanised, and asymmetric. Meanwhile, emerging threats such as the use of new technologies and artificial intelligence, misinformation, disinformation, and the presence of non-state actors, including private military and security companies, continue to change the way armed conflict is fought and the nature and scale of risks to civilians in conflict.

According to Amnesty International's Annual Report on Human Rights for 2023, released in Apr 2024, "The most powerful world powers, the United States, Russia, and China, have led a global disregard for international rules and values enshrined in the Universal Declaration of Human Rights, with civilians in conflicts paying the highest price". Agnes Callamard, Secretary General of Amnesty International, summarised that, "The level of violation of the international order witnessed in the past year was unprecedented". Each new conflict presents new ways belligerents rapidly adopt and use all available means and technologies, resulting in numerous humanitarian, legal, and ethical dilemmas. It indicates that the demands of numerous UNSC resolutions on PoC have gone largely unheeded.

Thus, armed conflicts in the contemporary world present increasingly complex challenges for PoC and the effective application of IHL. The current situation in various regions, including Africa, Ukraine, and Gaza, reinforces the essence and relevance of the IHL in preserving humanity. Against this backdrop, the topic is highly contemporary.

Moreover, this year holds special significance as it marks the 25th anniversary of UNSC Resolution 1265 (1999), which first established the PoC as a crucial issue of international peace and security, as well as the 75th anniversary of the Geneva Convention (1949), a cornerstone of IHL. Last week, several events were planned in New York on this critical issue as part of PoC Week 2024, alongside the UNSC Open Debate on PoC on 21 May 2024, which was also addressed by Ms. Mirjana Spoljaric Egger, President of the ICRC.

Opening Address

*Major General BK Sharma, AVSM, SM** (Retd)*
Director General, USI

Severe humanitarian atrocities are occurring in Afghanistan, Ukraine, Gaza, South Sudan, and other regions globally, with International Humanitarian Laws (IHL) being blatantly disregarded by both state and non-state actors. For the past three years, Afghanistan has been under the rule of the authoritarian Taliban regime, which lacks international legitimacy and recognition. The Taliban are oppressing women and persecuting their political opponents. About 97% of the population in Afghanistan is at the risk of facing famine or dying due to natural calamities. In Ukraine, due to the war, more than 3.7 million people are internally displaced and about 6.5 million refugees have moved to other countries. Further, extreme hardship is caused to the civil population due to the targeting of critical infrastructure and disruption of basic amenities of life. Likewise, in Gaza, more than 36,000 people have died due to military action, 75% of them were women and children. More than 80,000 people who have migrated to a confined space in the city of Rafah, are facing life and death situations on a daily basis. In Sudan, following the civil war, over 2.4 million people out of a population of 11 million have been internally displaced or have become refugees, with 65% of them being children. Acts of genocide are widespread in Southern Sudan. Ironically, the international community has become a helpless bystander, witnessing the drama of death and destruction day in and day out.

A farcical and regressive scenario is unfolding right now; the United Nations Security Council, the very custodian of the IHL, is deeply polarised and is incapable of upholding the tenets of the four Geneva Conventions and three additional protocols or for that matter implementing the resolutions of United Nations High Commission on Human Rights, or for that matter the verdicts passed by International Criminal Court and International Court of Justice. The vast divide in the comity of nations is evident from the voting on important United Nations resolutions on the protection of civilians in the ensuing conflicts. The nations have come to be seen to be categorised in four broad groups viz., tormentors, victims, duplicitous states and fence-sitters. There is scant debate on how to preserve and strengthen the IHL in the evolving anarchic scenario.

The growing trend of vitriolic conflicts reminds of Lee Kuan Yew's (founder of Singapore) prescient views that state behaviour will continue to be driven by social darwinism wherein, the primacy of national interests will remain paramount in hierarchical international order and ipso-facto, the use of force will remain central in achieving the balance of power in one's favour. Clearly, the strategic security landscape is characterised by a Volatility, Uncertainty, Complexity, and Ambiguity world, mired in ongoing conflicts, volatile flash points and critical uncertainties. In the recent past, the world has seen a number of 'Black Swan' events that have taken a heavy toll on civil population. Also, staring humanity in the eyes are 'Grey Rhinos' events (like climate change), ignoring which will cost dearly in terms of precious human lives and property. Regarding modern conflicts, the world has entered an era of new-generation warfare, characterised by significant changes in the nature and dynamics of conflicts.

Multi-domain wars and grey zone conflicts have become the order of the day. A new arms race, growing salience of weapons of mass destruction, and application of Artificial Intelligence and other disruptive technologies are radically ordering the character of war. The new generation of warfare is expanding to new strategic frontiers, including the use of Lethal Autonomous Weapon Systems, hyper-velocity vehicles, space, cyberspace, and the cognitive domain. This expansion compounds the challenges to the relevance and application of IHL. Therefore, there is a pressing need to understand the dynamics of a new generation of warfare, review, and refine peace building efforts, create more robust IHLs and attendant mechanisms for its enforcement.

India has a rich tradition of waging ethical wars, as depicted in the epics 'Ramayana' and 'Mahabharata', and in the scriptures of *Arthashastra* (The Science of Politics and Economics) and *Manusmriti* (The Laws of Manu, the progenitor of humanity). The treatment of 93,000 prisoners of war during the 1971 military campaign in Bangladesh, and subsequently, the humane treatment of Pakistani soldiers who lost their lives in the Kargil conflict, attest to India's strong commitment to and respect for IHL. The Indian Armed Forces are known for the use of minimum force and winning the hearts and minds of the civil population during counter-insurgency and counter-terrorism operations. Therefore, India is well poised to substantially contribute in the shaping the UN New Agenda for Peace-steeped in responsibility to protect civilians.

Keynote Address

Lieutenant General Rakesh Kapoor, AVSM, VSM
DCOAS (IS & C), Indian Army

1.　　Indeed, it is an honour to stand before you today and be a part of the USI-ICRC seminar on a very vital theme of ***Protection of Civilian in Modern Conflicts and International Humanitarian Law***. The theme for the seminar addresses critical issues affecting globally and that lie at the heart of international peace and security.

2.　　The lexicon and grammar of modern day conflict is changing. Trends over the last two decades show many armed conflicts prolong with no indication of resolution, and some are expanding. When we study the current Russo-Ukraine and Israel-Gaza conflict, the following trends emerge: -

　　(a)　　**<u>Duration</u>**. During Gulf war-I, conflicts were characterised precision guidance surgical strikes and meant to be short and decisive. The current conflicts while incorporate modern technologies and are in-fusing Revolution in Military Affairs (RMA), but the paradigm of duration is changing. We look at the Russo - Ukraine War, it started on 20 Feb 2022 and still continues after two years and 5 months. The Israel - Gaza, nine months since 07 Oct 2023 have passed and the conflict has not shown any signs of termination.

(b)   The other trend that may change is whether captured territories will be returned or retained by the captor and integrated with their own country. This may be the new normal. This trend has far reaching impact on future conflicts across the world.

(c)   **Technology is a Key Driver**. The symbiotic relationship between technology and doctrine was always a reality but is now becoming more profound. This in turn is increasing lethality, accuracy and making survivability equally challenging. The *Contact – Kinetic Phase* is possibly only one fourth of the conflict. While all other phases like the *Non-Contact – Non-Kinetic* are gaining more space in the landscape of conflicts. The players of these phases may be same or different. Current conflicts indicate multiple players from the uniformed soldier to the Geek sitting in a laboratory targeting your infrastructure and systems even before or simultaneously during the *Contact – Kinetic Phase*. So who is the civilian? How do we identify them? This question we all need to ask so as to how to identify the civilians who need protection under the International Humanitarian Law.

(d)   Recent conflicts also indicate adversarial nations trying to gain ascendency through narrative engineering and creation of effects. For creation of effects, you need targets that are appealing vis a vis some remote battlefield location. Where are these targets, they are either critical infrastructure or population centres. And this is where maximum civilians reside. Data shows that in the all the civil wars between 1989 and 2010, almost 50% of government forces and 60% of rebel groups deliberately attacked civilians. At the same time, known terrorist organisations carry out some of the most visible acts of civilian targeting to advance their political or ideological objectives. Civilians face enormous challenges trying to rebuild their neighbourhoods, economies and lives, with trauma persisting well beyond the conflict. And therefore, issue of protecting civilians comes up. Not just the physical protection but also the wherewithal to survive, in terms of food, water, shelter, medical facilities. And many of the civilian casualties are a result of the lack of these facilities. Alongside, is the trauma and consequential medical and psychological disorders faced by the surviving civilian population. One in five people living in active or recent war zones suffers from depression, anxiety, post-traumatic stress disorder (PTSD), bipolar disorder, or schizophrenia. As per UN data, due to the current conflicts, the *Ukraine War* has caused internal displacement of approx 3.7 million people, and in Gaza, 1.9 million people out of a population of 2.3 million.

(e)   Another trend that is being experienced in Armed Conflicts and civil wars, civilians are often used as tools of conflict. In Democratic Republic of Congo or South Sudan, population that is aligned or favours the adversarial group are deliberately targeted as punitive repudiation.

(f)   **<u>International Regulatory Bodies</u>**.

     (i)   *Where are the international bodies?*

     (ii)   *What role are they playing?*

     (iii)   *Who is listening to them?*

OR

Is it that some influential countries along with their close allies have created interest groups to manage and charter the trajectory of these conflicts as per their own economic, ideological or historical interests. This combined with the powerful social media, an info campaign is engineered that obscures the truth and at times the suffering of the civilian population, women, children, the old and infirm is obfuscated in conflicting narratives.

3.   Thus, the evolving nature of conflicts, the challenges faced on the ground, and the legal obligations that bind us must be unravelled. Discussions should seek to illuminate the way forward for the protection of civilian populations, including refugees and internally displaced persons, particularly women and children, and adherence to the principles of International Humanitarian Laws by warring parties. I think the way forward is that through robust and all pervasive International Humanitarian laws and status as rules that govern Armed conflicts. The existing Geneva conventions also need to be oriented to current times. To mitigate the challenges and provide succour, some of the steps that need to be taken are: -

(a)   **Decision Making**. International bodies like the UN Security Council, has to become more representative bringing forth the opinions and challenges faced by people across continents, regions, societies, ideologies and people. It cannot be the preserve of a selected few. This should be aligned and synchronised with current global dynamics. Certain defining parameters have to be enunciated to be part of the decision making body and should not represent the trends of the past.

(b)   **<u>Collective Responsibility and Collaboration</u>**. In 2005 during the 60th anniversary of the UN, member states unanimously accepted three inter-linked responsibilities constituting the principle of the Responsibility to Protect (R2P) based on three pillars: -

(i)   **<u>Pillar 1</u>**   Protection being a primary responsibility of the state. Each state has the responsibility to protect the population from genocide, war crimes, ethnic cleansing and crimes against humanity.

(ii)   **<u>Pillar 2</u>**   International Assistance and Capacity Building. States pledge to assist each other in their protection responsibilities.

(iii)   **<u>Pillar 3</u>**   Timely and Decisive Collective response. If any state is "manifestly failing" in its protection responsibilities, states should take collective action to protect the population.

(c)   Protection of Civilians (PoC) needs an integrated approach where the political, physical and enabling environment for the communities work in tandem. Host governments, local communities and humanitarian activists, all play essential roles in PoC. The framework exists, it is the implementation and the will to implement that is lacking.

(d)   Together, there is the opportunity to contribute to a safer, more just world for all. The decisions made, the knowledge gained, and the strategies formulated today directly impact the lives of countless individuals in conflict zones.

(e)   We understand, these are complex situations, but as responsible Nations, we need to find a way forward to make our planet liveable and preserve it for our future generations.

4.   To that extent, the USI has curated an excellent seminar with thought provoking sessions to improve the efficacy and credibility of International Humanitarian Laws and remove vulnerabilities that children, women and other civilians face as a result of conflicts raging across the globe.

5.   I once again express my gratitude to the USI for inviting me and giving me an opportunity to share some of my thoughts.

Special Address

Ms Ilze Brands Kehris
Assistant Secretary General, Human Rights and Head,
Office of the UN High Commissioner for Human Rights,
New York

Last year marked the 75th anniversary of the Universal Declaration of Human Rights. This year, the 75th anniversary of the 1949 Geneva Convention is being commemorated. These milestones emphasise the necessity of upholding International Humanitarian Law (IHL) and International Human Rights Law (IHRL).

Civilians bear the brunt of armed conflict, a reality increasingly highlighted by the outbreak of new conflicts and the escalation of existing ones. In 2023, the United Nations (UN) recorded at least 33,443 civilian deaths in armed conflicts, reflecting a 72% increase compared to 2022. The proportion of women and children killed doubled and tripled, respectively, compared to the previous year.

Armed conflicts are frequently marred by violations of IHRL and IHL by both state and non-state parties. Civilians suffer harm, forced displacement, destruction of infrastructure, deprivation of humanitarian aid, and even starvation, often appearing as intended consequences of the actions of conflict parties. Gaza has emerged as the deadliest conflict zone for civilians, aid workers, journalists, and UN personnel in recent years. In 2023, 70% of recorded deaths occurred in the occupied Palestinian territory and Israel, making it the deadliest conflict for civilians that year.

To date, according to the Gaza Ministry of Health, over 35,000 Palestinians have been killed and nearly 80,000 injured in Gaza, the vast majority being civilians. The actual numbers are likely to be higher. The use of explosive weapons with wide area effects in urban and populated areas, including missiles, artillery, mortars, and Improvised Explosive Devices (IEDs), are the primary causes of civilian deaths and injuries. These weapons also lead to the destruction of infrastructure, hospitals, schools, and neighbourhoods, severely impacting access to essential services like health, education, water, and housing, with long-lasting effects.

In Ukraine, the use of explosive weapons and IEDs with wide area effects have resulted in the majority of civilian casualties since the Feb 2022 invasion. More than 10,000 civilians have been killed, and over 21,000 injured. Over 1,600 medical and educational institutions have been destroyed or damaged. Millions have lost their homes and have been forced to flee.

New risks are also emerging with the military use of Artificial Intelligence (AI). The dangers posed by Lethal Autonomous Weapon Systems are recognised, with the UN Secretary-General calling for their prohibition. AI-driven decision, support and targeting systems are likely to have significant human rights impacts that have not yet been fully analysed, potentially leading to targeting practices that violate IHL principles.

Additionally, organised disinformation campaigns have added complexity to current conflict contexts. Disinformation, lacking a legal definition and varying in form, ranges from state-sponsored campaigns to conspiracy theories propagated by various actors. These campaigns significantly and broadly impact human rights, particularly during and relating to armed conflicts, further polarising societies and compounding existing discrimination and mistrust.

Non-compliance threatens peace and security, perpetuating violence. International organisations, civil society, and member states must intensify efforts to strengthen compliance with IHL and IHRL, ensuring accountability for violations. Accountability provides redress for victims and is crucial for breaking the cycle of impunity and preventing future conflicts.

There is an urgent need to increase the cost of non-compliance with international law to prevent future atrocities. The UN Secretary-General and the High Commissioner for Human Rights recently launched the UN Agenda for Protection, ensuring the protection of people in conflict, violence, and instability through the enjoyment of their human rights. Protection is not optional but a tactical imperative, reducing harm and perpetuating conflict and violence long after hostilities cease. It is part of a strategic, comprehensive, and preventative approach, addressing the root causes of conflict before it erupts.

The hope is that Member States will commit to this new approach in the upcoming pact of the future.

Special Address

Mr Kedir Awol Omar
Head of Regional Delegation for India, Nepal, Bhutan and the Maldives, ICRC, New Delhi

Countless civilians in conflicts around the world are experiencing the horrifying wrath of war. Any minute, the next missile can obliterate their home, their school, their hospitals and everyone in it. Any day, their loved ones might be abused, raped, detained, or tortured. Any week, they might run out of food or medicine.

Conflict is always bloody, and it ruins lives. In the logic of survival, room for humanity is difficult to find with the level of unprecedented violations. But it is precisely for these intractable circumstances that neutral and impartial humanitarian action was designed. International Humanitarian Law (IHL) provides minimum standards of humanity that must be respected in armed conflict. Its rules must be applied by all parties, irrespective of their motivation to go to war.

Today we are witnessing a decisive time for the world. Relationships between powerful states are strained, while multilateralism struggles to preserve its value and legitimacy in an atmosphere of division. States and media speak of larger-scale, international armed conflict almost as if they were inevitable. Nuclear weapons continue to threaten all of us. New ways of causing death and destruction are developed in lockstep with scientific advancements. While there is good reason to be concerned about a resurgence of conflict between states after a long period of mainly non-international armed conflicts, the established trends of the last two decades show no sign of letting up. Many non-international armed conflicts drag on, some of them worsening over time and devastating civilian lives and their properties. As our President stated recently in New York between 1999 and 2024 the number of active armed conflicts has increased from 20 to 120, which brought devastation to civilian lives and their properties.

Throughout 2023, hundreds of thousands of civilians were killed or suffered appalling injuries as victims of deliberate or indiscriminate attacks, as well as purportedly lawful attacks under IHL. The United Nations recorded as the Assistant Secretary General spoke earlier at least 33,443 civilian deaths in armed conflicts in 2023, a 72% increase as compared with 2022. The proportion of women and children killed doubled and tripled, respectively, as compared with 2022. In 2023, four out of every 10 civilians killed in conflicts were women, and three out of 10 were children.

As we have been witnessing daily the impact on civilians was particularly acute when fighting took place in populated urban areas and involved the use of explosive weapons. In 2023, almost 30,000 civilians were killed and injured by the use of explosive weapons in just six conflicts: Gaza, Myanmar, the Sudan, the Syrian Arab Republic, Ukraine and Yemen. Civilians accounted for 90% of those killed and injured when explosive weapons were used in populated areas.

As technology is rapidly developing, with cyber operations, autonomous weapons, and the use of outer space, questions regarding the application and interpretation of IHL are being raised. The overlapping effects of global financial pressures, rising inequalities, and the climate crisis make everything worse for civilians.

Another important factor in today's operating environment is misinformation and disinformation which also present a threat to populations and hinder humanitarian operations. Misinformation can fuel dangerous community divisions and undermine community acceptance of humanitarian organization and put their security at risk in their effort of delivering assistances, hence need to be addressed appropriately and timely.

For the ICRC, the issue of protection of civilians lies at the core of our mandate. As a neutral, impartial and independent organisation, we respond to the dire humanitarian needs and protection of the civilian population but engage also with parties to the conflict to reduce the effects of war by adhering to the basic humanitarian principles. When conflicts are characterised by widespread destruction and violation of IHL; then development and peace become an unachievable ambition. It is clear that the protection of civilians is a pre-condition or conduit for restoring stability, peace, and recovery, in addition to sparing the lives of civilians and their properties.

Despite these urgent and grave problems to address, we hold in our possession something extremely valuable: an international consensus. Every single state has signed the Geneva Conventions. Every state has freely and voluntarily agreed to be legally bound by the rules they embody. Every state has decided that no matter the circumstances that give rise to war, limiting its human cost is a legal obligation that cannot be swept aside. At a time when division hampers multilateralism, we must not underestimate the strength of the world's agreement on the basic rules of armed conflict. It is pertinent to highlight that this year, we commemorate the

75th anniversary of the Geneva Conventions, the background of today's gathering

ICRC is urging the states to elevate the laws of war to a political priority; to harness this unique consensus and to empower IHL to do the work it was meant to do at a moment in history when the worst has become too easily imaginable.

I must underscore that the protection of civilians means the protection of all. There is no chance of enduring stability or security until IHL is upheld for all genders.

Finally, I am sanguine that like today's high-level discussion and deliberations will be contributing to sensitisation of the subject matter further and shaping the valuable approaches to prevent and respond to violations of IHL and ensure the protection of civilians and their properties during armed conflicts. By fostering dialogue and collaboration, we aim to contribute to the efforts for ensuring compliance of IHL, ensuring a more secure and peaceful world, where the principles of human security and IHL are upheld, respected and humanity is preserved

I would like to take this opportunity to thank USI, Maj Gen B K Sharma, Maj Gen P K Goswami and the team for organising this important gathering.

I once again, thank you for being part of this important initiative and wish all participants and contributors great success.

Session I: Protection of Civilians in Modern Conflicts and International Humanitarian Law

Chair – Lieutenant General JS Lidder, UYSM, AVSM (Retd)
Former Force Commander and Subsequently Deputy
Special Representative of the Secretary-General (Political),
Sudan

Opening Remarks

Contemporary conflicts have brought unprecedented levels of death and destruction, making the PoC an increasingly complicated endeavour. Traditional methods of protection are proving less effective in the face of these modern challenges. In the first session, there will be discussions on the key trends and challenges in protecting civilians in contemporary conflicts, particularly within the purview of IHL compliance.

Modern conflicts are defined by four critical issues: prolonged durations with high intensity of force, systematic targeting of population centres, forced displacement by attrition and the denial of humanitarian needs, and the cyber weaponisation of conflict. Regrettably, these actions are often justified as necessary for achieving operational victories and objectives of war at any cost. The complexity and brutality of these conflicts necessitate re-evaluating the approaches to civilian protection.

Over the last two years, there has been a severe undermining of IHL by both state and non-state armed groups. Ironically, these actors seem to have a near-absence of moral obligation and institutional accountability. This disregard for IHL principles has exacerbated the suffering of civilians and has highlighted the urgent need for reinforced legal and ethical standards in warfare.

Despite this unfortunate situation, there are inspiring stories of determined protective measures being adopted by local and international humanitarian workers, including those from the ICRC. These individuals work in hazardous environments such as Gaza, Ukraine, and Sudan, demonstrating exceptional courage and commitment. Their efforts remind us of the potential for positive impact even in the most dire circumstances. It is imperative that stakeholders emulate the dedication shown by others by finding new, meaningful, and urgent ways to protect civilians in modern conflicts.

Trends In Modern Conflicts

Dr Ajai Sahni
Executive Director, The Institute for Conflict Management

A Crisis of Faith

Today's crisis of global institutions and law is one of faith, trust and legitimacy. These institutions, far from reflecting the consensual opinion of their diverse memberships, have been captured by great power alliances, subordinated by financial pressures from their major donors, and manipulated and blackmailed by strident cabals. Worse, they are instrumentalised by dominant powers, used against their perceived ideological adversaries, and ignored even when near-unanimous opinion stands in the way of the geo-strategic ambitions of these powers. The veto, intended to provide a balance against any tyranny of majorities or alliances, has been exercised without reference to any ethical framework. The 'Rule-Based Order' that the West propagates is meant only for others and cannot bind the club of Western states.

Since the beginning of the present century (and indeed long before it), the Western powers, led by the USA, have rampaged across the world, devastating nations, promoting domestic instability and civil war, causing death, maiming, and displacement of hundreds of millions, without recourse to any countervailing action by international institutions. These institutions and laws have essentially been used against weak states arbitrarily targeted by the Western powers, rather than against the most egregious offenders in the world. Within such a context, any discussion of IHL and PoC can only be an academic exercise. Unless international institutions undergo radical reform, a prospect that remains uncertain – to ensure equitable compliance, the content and formulation of the laws themselves can only serve, at best, as appeals to good conduct, but are more likely to lapse into postures of piety.

The Nature and Character of War

Since Clausewitz (Prussian general and military theorist), the accepted wisdom has been that, while the character of war changes constantly with technology, strategy and tactical inventiveness, the nature of war is a constant, defined by armed violence. This maxim, however, is being progressively challenged. While most elements of contemporary war have echoes or roots in history, such as proxy operations, economic, social, and political disruption in enemy states, disinformation and influence operations, espionage, subversion, sabotage, etc., the sheer scale and impact of these interventions, enabled by contemporary technologies, have led to fundamental transformations, prompting a significant shift in the understanding of war. The boundaries of war and peace have been blurred, even as non-military means have become more important, and at least potentially more disruptive and lethal, than military means, so much so that many argue that the former should now be seen as patterns of violence. These patterns have created a tremendous capacity to inflict harm on target states, and specifically on their civilian populations.

There has, however, been no authoritative shift in the definition of war as armed violence or the threat thereof. The danger or realisation of armed attack remains the basis of international and national laws that regulate conflict. This has created a far-reaching disjunction between contemporary international legislation and the realities on the ground, leaving little possibility of legal recourse to victims of a range of potentially destructive, even lethal, interventions that do not meet the definition of armed conflict.

The Western powers, led by the US, continue to opportunistically adhere to the traditional concept of the nature of war, claiming that their numerous actions across continents are 'Operations short of war,' 'Non-military measures', and indeed 'Ways to avoid war'. These include, among other things, the many 'Colour Revolutions' that the West has sponsored, sanctions, 'Democracy Promotion', and information and cyber operations, as well as covert operations, including targeted assassinations and support to extremist, militant, and terrorist proxies.

One of the prominent target states, and itself a frequent offender, Russia, however, increasingly views these as acts of war and insists that the understanding of war must go beyond armed violence. Thus, sanctions, colour revolutions, information, and cyber manipulation are all viewed as attempts to engineer regime change and mount economic, information, and hybrid wars.

While the West formally continues to adhere to the Clausewitzian framework, there is a visible shift towards a more complex understanding of war. President Joe Biden has indicated that a cyber-attack may be considered an act of war, declaring that if the US ends up in "A real shooting war with a major power, it's going to be as a consequence of a cyber breach of great consequence". Unsurprisingly, the US Defence Department has declared cyberspace a new 'Domain of Warfare'.

The Revolution in Armed Violence

Technology has also transformed critical elements of the character of armed violence that have a far-reaching impact on the security of civilian populations. Among these is the shift of the locus of war from borders and peripheries to population centres, towns and cities, the radical contraction of the response time frame, increasing uncertainty and the mounting risk of unintended escalation. While modern wars were, for some time, imagined to be 'Short, Swift and Decisive', the experience of the wars of the 21st Century has demonstrated that such a conceptualisation was sheer fantasy, as most of the conflicts of the present age have tended to protraction, and have had devastating consequences for civilian populations. Earl Tilford thus wrote of the 'Short War Delusion' and warned that one was engaged in what can accurately be described as a 'Protracted, Attritional, Global struggle'.

As Artificial Intelligence, autonomous machine systems, drones and drone swarms, robots, lasers and, potentially, biological weapons are progressively harnessed for the purposes of war, this trajectory can only accelerate, and the impact on civilian populations can only be even more overwhelming.

While technological asymmetries appear to confer overwhelming advantages on technologically advanced powers, technologically disadvantaged entities have been seen to adapt, adopting alternative strategies and measures: terrorism, a shift into the urban terrain, the use of human shields, propaganda and information campaigns, cyber-campaigns, among others, to counter the technological advantages of the dominant powers.

A brief focus on human shields is perhaps in order here. This is a tactic that has been widely used in conflicts. Still, two examples stand out in scale, the use of human shields by the Sri Lankan terrorist group, the Liberation Tigers of Tamil Eelam in 2009, and the current adoption of this tactic by Hamas in Gaza. The former failed in the face of the determined onslaught of the Sri Lankan security forces. However, this drew the opprobrium of international bodies, particularly leading Western states, which continue to hound Sri Lanka for 'Justice'. In Gaza, the tactic appears to be securing significant current success, as the war of perceptions has turned significantly against the massive loss and disruption of civilian lives in Israeli operations, with minor commentary focusing on the cynical and overwhelming employment of human shields and the location of Hamas units and firepower in the most densely populated areas, including locations such as hospitals, schools and mosques, many of which are also used as overcrowded civilian shelters for the millions whom Israel's campaigns have displaced. It is not sufficient to dismiss Hamas as a terrorist group and continue to exert international pressure on Israel alone. Suppose the use of human shields proves to be even a partially successful tactic in this situation, allowing Hamas to survive and recover some of its political heft. In that case, this will inevitably tempt other groups to adopt similar devices. IHL and institutions and procedures for the PoC will have to grapple with the harsh realities of this predicament.

As one looks towards the sixth generation of warfare, it is helpful to recall that 'Fourth Generation Warfare' has already, and indeed, repeatedly, defeated the world's 'Sole Superpower'. With their broad overlap with civilian technologies, sixth-generation technologies offer weaker entities a range of instrumentalities that can help balance out at least some of the asymmetries that confer an advantage on the great(er) powers, even as these inflict enormous financial costs on the latter. Thus, for instance, as has been widely noted, the 9/11 attacks cost their perpetrators between USD 4,00,000 and 5,00,000. The US 'War on Terrorism' has cost over USD 8 tn. Moreover, after spending more than USD 300 mn a day in Afghanistan for 20 years, US was still confronted with a profound and humiliating failure. These are exemplars for future warfare and will tempt powers, greater and lesser, to operate below the threshold of armed conflict or, during armed conflict, to act within the formulation of protracted wars that seek to avoid direct and decisive confrontations.

Unrestricted Wars

These transformations impose new strategic and organisational challenges on the world's countries. In China and the concept of 'Unrestricted Warfare,' one can find perhaps the most thorough adaptations at present. The People's Liberation Army (PLA) conceptualises '7 Wars': missile, drone, invisible (cyber and electromagnetic spectrum), space, land, sea and air. In its latest reforms of Apr 2024, the structure of the PLA came to comprehend four services, land, air, sea and rocket force; and four arms, aerospace force; cyberspace force, joint logistics theatre force and the information support force. China, moreover, recognises and provides institutional structures for another '3 Warfare', lawfare, public opinion, psychological and financial warfare.

These, however, do not exhaust China's unrestricted warfare instrumentalities. A wide range of government-backed initiatives exploit smuggling, market disruption, culture wars, drug wars, information, media and fabrication warfare, technological warfare (gaining control of or having an edge in particular vital technologies that can be used in both peace and wartime; the capture of critical and rare earths); environmental warfare, terrorism, and political subversion are elements that are explicitly envisaged. According to the paradigm of 'Unrestricted Warfare', there are no rules;

nothing is forbidden and civilian technologies are employed as military weapons 'Without Morality'. Within such a framework, one must understand that non-military means can be as effective as a nuclear weapon.

Crucially, moreover, as the adversary pursues 'Cross-domain coercion', and the preferred objective is to keep its own soldiers 'Outside the Battlespace' and to destroy the enemy's economic potential, administrative institutions and socio-political cohesion, the consequences for civilian populations can, and have been catastrophic. This is more than visible in the wars in Ukraine and Gaza that are presently overwhelmingly projected in the global media, but are also the case, in varying measures, in other contemporary conflicts.

A Global Regression

As the old-world order crumbles, there has been a widespread regression from civilised norms, from the aspiration to civilisation. Political cultures everywhere are veering towards authoritarianism, while international affairs incline increasingly to the primitive rule of brute force. One is again at a moment of global dysfunction and uncertainty where established powers, unwilling to relinquish long habits of dominance and exceptionalism, are challenged by a rising adversary, even as lesser players exploit the uncertainties of the age to smash and grab wherever the opportunity presents itself.

Within such an environment, a tremendous reassertion of ethical and just norms may succeed in re-establishing some international authority exercised to protect civilians and reassert the importance of IHL. It is often noted that there is little will for such a re-assertion. The more significant problem is that, among those who matter most, it is not just the will lacking, but the desire itself.

Challenges to the Protection of Civilians in Modern Conflicts

Lieutenant General Mohan Subramanian, PVSM, AVSM, SM, VSM

Force Commander, United Nations Mission in South Sudan

Introduction

Mr Dag Hammarskjold, the second Secretary-General of the United Nations (UN), once remarked, "The UN was not created to take mankind to heaven but to save humanity from hell". In today's conflict scenarios, this 'Hell' refers to the plight of helpless civilians caught in armed conflict zones. For this reason, former Secretary-General, Mr Ban Ki-Moon identified the Protection of Civilians (PoC) as the defining purpose of the UN in the 21st Century. The PoC has thus become an overarching priority for most UN Peacekeeping Missions (UNPKM), wherein, all available resources and capacities are prioritised for PoC.

Challenges of the Protection of Civilians and Mitigating Measures

Intangible Impact of Conflict Prevention Efforts of Missions. Ideally, conflict prevention would be the most effective way to protect civilians. While leadership and community engagement are essential tools towards this end, enhancing the mission's footprint by increasing the number of peacekeeping bases and density of troops on the ground side by side is equally important. Extensive deployment of peacekeepers will be able to protect more civilians and even though is cost-intensive, will be worth the cost. Usually, casualties to civilians are considered as a parameter to judge the effectiveness of peace operations, which can be misleading and make a dent in the credibility of the peacekeeping mission. Therefore, constituting special teams to take stock of the number of lives saved would be worthwhile for the field missions to boost peacekeepers' morale, motivate them to perform better, and serve as a valuable measure of effectiveness.

Mandates. Multi-functional mandates raise expectations in the local communities. However, when the mandate or part of it is not implemented, it results in frustration and loss of hope. Thus, challenges related to PoC mandates should be addressed at the levels of the UN Headquarters/UN Security Council.

Success or failure of UNPKM. The closure of peace operations in Mali and Democratic Republic of Congo is not an indication of the failure of The United Nations Multidimensional Integrated Stabilization Mission in Mali and The United Nations Organization Stabilization Mission in the Democratic Republic of the Congo. Because there are factors that affected the performance of the mission, which were beyond the control of either the peacekeepers or the mission.

Managing Consent of Host Government. The success of peace operations depends on the consent of the host state. When the consent is either withdrawn or diluted or when the host state considers the peacekeeping mission a liability, implementation of the mandate becomes a challenge.

Are Resources the Panacea for Problems Faced by the Protection of Civilians? For the PoC mandates, there should be adequate resources, but it does not imply that all steps taken to protect civilians will be successful. Resources are essential to match the requirement but not excessive.

The mindset of Uniformed and Civilian Peacekeepers. People who have been involved in peacekeeping for a few decades now, both military and civilian peacekeepers, have developed a risk-averse, non-proactive mindset. It needs to be replaced with one that is dynamic and responsive.

Caveats. Mission and force leadership needs complete freedom to make appropriate operational decisions without being burdened by caveats. Declared/undeclared caveats by Troop/Police Contributing Countries, if any, may also derail PoC effectiveness like the withdrawal of the Belgium Battalion from Rwanda at the onset of the 1994 genocide.

Freedom of Movement. Limiting the freedom of movement of the peacekeepers impedes their operational effectiveness. The mission, therefore must put in place a mechanism to engage with the host government to ensure freedom of movement to the peacekeepers.

Decision Dilemma on Prioritising Protection of Civilians Efforts by Ground Commanders. Responding to threats to civilians can create a decision dilemma since it is not possible to respond to every situation simultaneously. Given the large area of operation and the need to respond quickly, the onus to make such a decision falls on the shoulders of relatively junior commanders on the ground. For example, during the conflict in the Upper Nile State in South Sudan from Sep to Nov 2022, instead of embroiling in the conflict between White Army Nuers and Shilluk Armed Factions in the affected villages, a decision was taken to strongly defend Kodok Village, which was perhaps the next objective for attack by the Nuer White Army. In another conflict in the Greater Pibor Administrative Area in South Sudan in Dec 2022, a decision was taken to protect the corridor of civilians fleeing from the area of conflict and strongly defend Pibor, which was probably the next objective for attack by Nuer youth and where over 17,200 Internally Displaced Persons (IDP) had gathered. In the case of clashes in Malakal PoC Camp on 08 Jun 2023, the United Nations Mission in South Sudan (UNMISS) Force interposed quick reaction teams in between clashing communities, segregated them and contained the clashes. Irrespective of the option chosen, there can be criticism in hindsight on why the other options were not exercised. Since UNPKMs often do not have the adequate resources to simultaneously respond to all threats to civilians, the responses will have to be prioritised.

Inadequate Peacekeeping Intelligence (PKI) and Early Warning (EW). Intelligence gathering is taboo in the UN because it is considered intrusive. The resultant non-availability of early warning is a limiting factor for the peacekeepers' response to the call to protect civilians.

Gap Between Early Warning and Early Actions (EA). The absence of the right mindset of peacekeepers, both uniformed and civilian, the inadequacy of the right kind of air and surface mobility resources, inadequate training, and deficiencies in leadership lead to a gap between EW and EA, in both temporal and physical domains. It cripples the PoC strategy. 'Staying ahead of the curve' is the *mantra* to ensure proactive PoC.

Continuity of Tenures - Institutional Knowledge. The rotation of uniformed peacekeepers, generally in a year, seriously dents the continuity and availability of institutional knowledge, which are critical for PoC effectiveness.

Gap Between Situational Awareness (What) and Situational Understanding (Why and How). While many briefs and inputs provide situational awareness, lack of continuity, absence of institutional/background knowledge and lack of civil-military integration militate against the situational understanding that is critically important for effective PoC.

Mis/Dis/Mal-Information. Mis/Dis/Mal-information campaigns by the rebel groups are a formidable obstacle to the mission's ability to disseminate the truth. It in turn kills transparency and shows the peacekeepers in a poor light. Keeping the international partners and other stakeholders including the host government informed helps to face this challenge.

Lack of Integrated Use of Technology. Currently, the mission lacks the wherewithal to maintain an integrated database, which is vital for the operational planning of the mission.

PoC without Weapons. The lives of civilians are sometimes protected physically by UNPKM without taking recourse to arms/weapons. The worst floods in sixty years have impacted Bentiu town in Unity State, South Sudan, leaving it virtually submerged except few patches of land remaining above water level. The country's largest concentration of IDPs, over 1,70,000, is located here. Peacekeepers of UNMISS and UN partners constructed over 25 km of earthen dykes around the town. Patrols of UNMISS monitored the dykes 24x7 to detect breaches and on the occurrence, fix them expeditiously to prevent flooding of the IDP Camps and the city. On 07 and 08 Oct 22, one such breach was detected by a patrol, which expanded to 21 m in width and 9 m in depth within 30 minutes. Heavy engineering equipment could not reach the breach and water gushed into IDP camp areas. Without loss of time, over 2,000 peacekeepers filled sandbags, carried them on foot and fixed the breach by continuously working for 36 to 48 hours. This saved the lives of nearly 40,000 IDPs who were elderly, infirm, or children, unable to move and at risk of drowning in the deluge. Such actions are regularly taken by the peacekeepers as a natural response to climate change calamities.

Integrated Vs Joint/Co-located Functioning. While different components of a Mission may be co-located and may function jointly but may not be functioning in an integrated manner. Integration implies trust and respect for each other backed up by a seamless flow of information laterally and not only in vertical silos or stow pipes. In this regard, in most missions, there is much ground to cover.

Static Vs Mobile Posture. Adequate force protection measures outside and inside the base are necessary to mitigate the threat of violence to the peacekeepers. However, apportioning sizeable resources towards static security duties to protect bases/airstrips/critical installations, reduces the availability of troops for mobile operations. There is a need to continuously review and reduce boots on static duties to enhance the effectiveness of the implementation of the protection mandate. Optimal use of technology will help reduce the static responsibilities to some extent, which, however, implies an adequate infusion of technology and an increased budget for the mission.

Inadequate Women Peacekeepers. Since women and children are the main victims of violence, women peacekeepers and their ability to strike a rapport with the vulnerable community is an asset to the mission. Currently, the number of women peacekeepers deployed is far less than the desired number.

How much Integration is Useful? Integration is very often talked of as a rule. Sometimes, integration can result in a specialist job undertaken by a non-specialist agency because everything is to be integrated. On the other hand, decision-making can be delayed because developing a consensus to arrive at an integrated decision, is time-consuming. Hence specific critical tasks should be best left to the specialists. Integration is the way to go but determining where integration is essential and where it can be counterproductive will be the key to productive integration.

International Humanitarian Law and Challenges of Modern Armed Conflict

Dr George Dvaladze
Regional Legal Advisor for South Asia, ICRC, Delhi

Introduction

The International Committee for Red Cross (ICRC) is an impartial, humanitarian, and neutral humanitarian organisation that provides protection and assistance to the civilian population affected by armed conflict and other situations of violence with the purpose of alleviating their suffering.

Neutrality, as the underlying principle of ICRC's action, implies that the organisation generally does not publicly pronounce itself to denounce violations that occur in armed conflicts; instead, it engages in bilateral, confidential and constructive dialogue with all parties to address shortcomings in respect for the law, as well as challenges posed. Nevertheless, once every four years, and on the occasion of the International Conference of the Red Cross and Red Crescent (International Conference), the ICRC publishes a report on 'IHL and the Challenges of Contemporary Armed Conflicts'[5] (Challenges Report). In these reports, the ICRC provides perspectives and insights on over 120 armed conflicts worldwide, highlighting the major challenges posed by contemporary armed conflicts for IHL. The aim is to stimulate broader reflection on these challenges and outline current or prospective ICRC actions, positions, and areas of interest.

The last edition of the Challenges Report, published in 2019, provides a catalogue of various challenges in modern conflict, which serves as a reference for the panel discussion. It is noteworthy that the next edition of the report will be published later this year (2024), ahead of the 34th edition of the International Conference which shall take place in the month of Oct 2024.

The 2019 Challenges Report refers to the following topics:

- **Urbanisation of Warfare**. The PoC against the effects of hostilities, the use of explosive weapons in populated areas, and the PoC during sieges.

- **New Technologies of Warfare**. Cyber operations during armed conflict; autonomous weapon systems; artificial intelligence and machine learning; the potential use of weapons in outer space, and legal reviews of new weapon systems.

- **The needs of civilians in increasingly long conflicts**. The protection of Internally Displaced Persons, the protection of persons with disabilities, and access to education during armed conflict.

- **IHL and Non-State Armed Groups (NSAGs)**. The applicability of IHL to conflicts with multiple NSAGs, the protection of persons living in territory controlled by NSAGs, and detention by NSAGs.

- **Terrorism, Counter-Terrorism Measures, and IHL**. The applicability of IHL to fighting 'Terrorism' and NSAGs designated as terrorists;

counter-terrorism measures and principled humanitarian action; and the status and protection of foreign fighters and their families.

• **Climate, Armed Conflict, and the Natural Environment**. The effects of conflict on climate and the environment; the revised ICRC 'Guidelines for the Protection of the Natural Environment in Situations of Armed Conflict'.

• **Enhancing respect for IHL**. Guidelines on investigations in armed conflict; its 'Roots or Restraint in War' study; its work on 'Support Relationships', and its platform on 'IHL in Action'.

Urbanisation of Warfare

Erosion of respect for IHL remains a significant challenge that the international community, including states and other relevant actors, must continue to address. In response to this pressing issue, the 35th International Conference will focus on a draft resolution titled 'Towards a Universal Culture of Compliance with International Humanitarian Law'. States and national societies of the Red Cross and Red Crescent have been invited to provide their input on the draft resolution.

To set the background for the discussion on challenges related to urban warfare, a video that highlighted the devastating chain reaction urban combat has on civilians, was shown to the audience. This video illustrated the cascading effects of damage to infrastructure in urban warfare, like hospitals, homes, businesses, power grids and water treatment plants, which disrupt essential services and trigger a flight of skilled professionals. Consequently, food supply chains, communication, and cleanliness are severely hampered. The desperation brought on by unfulfilled bomb threats and a shortage of basic supplies leads to a state of starvation, illness, and disintegration of families.

The damage goes beyond the immediate conflict. Safety nets, social cohesiveness, and public health are all undermined by this slow, sneaky spiral. To break the spiral, governments and armed actors must prioritise the protection of civilians in all urban military operations in their doctrine, training, and planning for urban operations. This protection of civilians must be reflected in their conduct. This obligation is clear under the IHL.[6]

ICRC's report on 'War in Cities: Preventing and Addressing the Humanitarian Consequences for Civilians'[7] outlines the large-scale, complex consequences of armed conflict for urban populations as unacceptable. As the world urbanises, so do the conflicts. In recent times, conflicts have increasingly been taking place in cities and other areas characterised by concentrations of civilians and civilian objects. This trend is likely to continue. Armed conflict has specific, large-scale, multi-faceted effects on urban communities and infrastructure. Protecting people from harm means more than just preventing death and physical injury. Much suffering is interrelated, is not immediately visible and is long-lasting. Those responsible urgently need to gain a deeper understanding of the complex and accumulated patterns of civilian harm involved. A change of mindset is crucial, as parties to the conflict must accept their responsibility for minimising the suffering of civilians, whose protection must be at the centre of those parties, policies and practices.

New Technologies of Warfare

Modern conflicts that take place in cities and other populated areas are often fought using weapons designed to deliver large explosive force from afar and over large areas. Many, if not all, of these heavy explosive weapons are ill-adapted for use in urban and other population centres. When employed in populated areas, where targets are often intermingled with civilians or civilian objects, such weapons are likely to have indiscriminate effects, with devastating consequences for civilian populations.

According to the ICRC's Report, 'Explosive Weapon with Wide Area Effects: A Deadly Choice in Populated Areas'[8], confirms that the use of explosive weapons with a wide impact area in populated areas is one of the main causes of civilian harm in today's armed conflicts. The ICRC has witnessed this pattern of harm in recent and ongoing armed conflicts in over fifteen contexts, including Afghanistan, Gaza, Iraq, Libya, Philippines, Somalia, Sri Lanka and Yemen.

When explosive weapons with a wide impact area are used in populated areas, the overwhelming majority of the casualties are civilians. Bombing and shelling have wounded and killed large numbers of people and permanently disabled many others, especially in areas where healthcare is inadequate or inaccessible. They also cause serious long-term psychological trauma among countless others, particularly children. Cities, including civilian housing, critical infrastructure, schools, and places of worship, are reduced to rubble.

These devastating consequences are long-lasting. When critical infrastructure is hit, services indispensable to the survival of the population i.e., water, sanitation, electrical power, and healthcare are disrupted and may even collapse. Lack of essential services seriously endangers the lives and well-being of civilians and may lead to outbreaks of disease and even epidemics. These 'Reverberating' effects can spread far in time and space and can affect a much larger part of the civilian population than those in the impact zone of the attack. Women and children are particularly vulnerable in specific ways.

The damage and destruction caused by heavy explosive weapons trigger displacement, forcing survivors to flee and expose themselves to an array of new risks, prevent the return of displaced populations and can have a significant impact on the natural environment; all this is compounded by the presence of unexploded ordnance, that keep on killing long after hostilities have ended. Ultimately, the use of heavy explosive weapons in cities and other populated areas significantly undermines the achievement of the Sustainable Development Goals.

Enhancing Respect for IHL

There is no general prohibition under the IHL against using heavy explosive weapons in populated areas; however, such use must comply with all the rules governing the conduct of hostilities, notably the prohibitions against indiscriminate and disproportionate attacks and the obligation to take all feasible precautions in attack.

Because of their low accuracy and precision and their large destructive radius relative to the size of most military objectives in populated areas, when used in such environments, many heavy explosive weapons are likely to have indiscriminate effects. This casts doubt on whether such weapons can, in a populated environment, be directed against a specific military objective and whether their effects can be limited as required by the IHL to comply with the prohibition against indiscriminate attacks.

The IHL requires parties to armed conflict to consider the direct and indirect effects of an attack, death or injury of civilians, or damage to civilian objects, in particular. While the indirect and reverberating effects of heavy explosive weapons' use in populated areas are well documented and foreseeable, it is doubtful whether parties appropriately factor them into their assessment of the lawfulness of such use. The humanitarian and legal imperative to protect the civilian population requires the taking measures to limit the wide-area effects of weapons, or otherwise reduce the risk to civilians, or using alternative weapons or tactics.

The extent of civilian harm caused by the use of heavy explosive weapons in populated areas, as witnessed by the ICRC and others, raises serious questions about how parties to conflict interpret and apply these key rules of the IHL that aim to protect civilians. It also demonstrates the difficulty of using heavy explosive weapons in populated areas in compliance with the IHL.

The ICRC is calling for the use of heavy explosive weapons in populated areas to be avoided as a matter of policy. A policy of avoidance means that heavy explosive weapons should not be used in populated areas unless sufficient mitigation measures are taken to limit their wide area effects and the consequent risk of civilian harm. To be effective, such an avoidance policy should entail the adoption of concrete preventive measures and guidance (policies and practices) to be put in place in advance of armed conflicts and military operations and faithfully implemented when planning and conducting hostilities in populated areas. Such measures should be shared with partner forces or supported parties and taken into consideration when deciding on the transfer of heavy explosive weapons and when providing support to a party to an armed conflict.

Among the initiatives to address this challenge is the adoption of a 'Political declaration on strengthening the PoC from the humanitarian consequences arising from the use of explosive weapons in populated areas'.[9] It is not an ICRC led initiative, but instead a state-led initiative; nevertheless, the ICRC strongly supports the initiative and encourages states who have not done so to sign the document and to take steps for its implementation. As of today, 83 states have already signed the document, including states from the Indo-Pacific region.

Summing-Up

Chair – Lieutenant General JS Lidder, UYSM, AVSM (Retd)
Former Force Commander and Subsequently Deputy
Special Representative of the Secretary-General (Political),
Sudan

The nature of war has evolved, presenting a range of physical, cyber, and moral threats. Consequently, the operating environment for protecting civilians has introduced new challenges that must be analysed and adapted to ensure adequate protection measures. This shift necessitates re-examining the strategies and methodologies in response to these multifaceted threats.

There is an increasing mistrust in international organisations, which requires urgent attention and remedy. The UNSC, in particular, needs immediate reforms to restore the UN's institutional credibility. However, until these structural changes are implemented, modifications should be made to allow for broader consultations and collaborative decision-making processes. This will ensure that stakeholders from conflict-affected regions have a voice in the proceedings.

We must encourage comprehensive political dialogue that includes non-state and private players. Strengthening international and national accountability systems with stringent legal obligations is crucial to ensure that those responsible for violations are held accountable. Such measures will enhance the credibility and effectiveness of efforts to protect civilians.

An integrated approach is essential for the physical protection of civilians and the coordination of emergent humanitarian aid. Building cyber resilience is also critical, which includes implementing credible strategic communications and countering fake news and hate narratives. This holistic approach will help address the diverse challenges posed by modern conflicts.

The discussion and application of a ban on the use of technology-driven autonomous weapons are necessary. Additionally, militaries should engage in joint training with political and humanitarian actors to operate within the IHL provisions. This collaboration aims to mitigate collateral damage in urban warfare and enhance overall civilian protection.

National commitments to protecting civilians must be strengthened. It is vital to incorporate communities in dialogue, humanitarian access, healthcare, self-protection measures, and combating climate emergencies. Investments are needed to build local capacities and capabilities, ensuring that national authorities can effectively protect civilians. By fostering these comprehensive and inclusive approaches, stakeholders can better address the complexities of modern conflicts and enhance the PoC.

Session II: Responding to Challenges of Modern Conflicts

Chair - Dr George Dvaladze,
Regional Legal Advisor for South Asia, ICRC, Delhi

Opening Remarks

The continuous evolution of the world is reflected in the nature of armed conflicts, marked by the perpetual transformation humanity undergoes, be it technological advancements or changes in human interaction. The novelty in various aspects characterising modern conflicts necessitates understanding how existing rules and principles designed to regulate the behaviour of actors in armed conflict should be interpreted and applied to address humanitarian issues and concerns.

The IHL, also referred to as the law of armed conflict, restricts the freedom of belligerents to use force, aiming to protect civilian populations from the harmful effects of armed conflict. These rules and principles regulate both traditional and modern means and methods of warfare. However, clarity and nuance are often required to understand better how these existing rules must be interpreted and applied to address the challenges of contemporary conflicts.

Technological development continues to expand the boundaries of warfare. Recent conflicts have already showcased some critical features of these advancements, and their use is expected to only increase in the future, bringing both positive and negative consequences for civilian protection. Particularly deserving of attention are the potential human costs of cyber warfare and the legal and ethical issues related to the loss of human control over the use of force due to autonomy in the 'Critical Functions' of weapon systems.

In recent conflicts, the use of digital technology beyond conventional means and methods of warfare has significantly impacted civilian populations. For instance, misinformation, disinformation campaigns, and online propaganda have proliferated on social media, leading to heightened tensions and violence against and between communities. While disinformation and surveillance are not unique or new to armed conflicts, the extensive reach and force-multiplying effect provided by digital technology can exacerbate and add to the existing vulnerabilities of those affected by armed conflicts.

Multi-national forces, including United Nations peacekeepers, continue to be deployed in volatile contexts, including armed conflict settings and are often entrusted with the duty of protecting civilian populations. The shift from traditional duties to broader mandates, along with their deployment in increasingly violent contexts, results in greater risk and a higher likelihood of these forces being called upon to use force and becoming implicated in armed conflict situations. Therefore, clarity regarding the legal regime applicable to such forces and the expectations placed upon them remains essential to ensure their ability to protect civilian populations effectively.

Humanitarian concerns and challenges related to the IHL arise with operations conducted by all parties to armed conflicts. However, specific issues present themselves differently, particularly concerning non-state armed groups. It is crucial to reflect upon the applicability of the IHL to situations involving multiple armed groups, the legal regime protecting civilians living in territories under the de facto control of these groups, and how to enhance respect for the IHL by all parties involved in the conflict, including non-state armed groups.

In a previous session, speakers shared valuable insights on modern warfare's legal, practical, and humanitarian challenges and offered concrete proposals for responding to these challenges. This session highlights selected issues particularly relevant to the challenges posed by modern conflicts, including new warfare technologies such as cyber operations, artificial intelligence and machine learning, and autonomous weapon systems. Additionally, issues such as misinformation, disinformation, and hate speech, significantly amplified by modern technology, and the increasing involvement of non-state armed groups in conflicts is discussed. These deliberations and inputs will significantly contribute to the collective effort to preserve humanity in contemporary conflicts.

By examining these insights and proposals, stakeholders can better navigate the complexities of modern warfare and ensure that the IHL continues to provide robust protection for those affected by armed conflicts. Through such renewed understanding and collective action, it is possible to uphold the principles of humanity in the face of evolving warfare.

Challenges of Misinformation, Disinformation, Malinformation and Hate Speech - Impact on Protection of Civilians and Peacekeepers

Dr Andrew E. Yaw Tchie
Senior Fellow, Norwegian Institute of International Affairs

Introduction

Recent developments in UN peacekeeping missions reveal significant challenges posed by Misinformation, Disinformation, Malinformation (MDM), and hate speech. A recent report by the Effectiveness of Peacekeeping Operations Network examines these issues in the contexts of South Sudan, the Democratic Republic of the Congo (DRC), and the Central African Republic (CAR). An attempt has been made to understand the broader implications of MDM on peacekeeping operations and the ways in which these missions are impacted and respond to these challenges.

Misinformation and disinformation are particularly prevalent around election periods, critical junctures, or during the signing of agreements. These periods often coincide with significant state challenges, making them ripe for the spread of false information. In South Sudan, the DRC, and the CAR, these dynamics exacerbate existing tensions and create additional hurdles for peacekeeping efforts. The spread of MDM during these times has led to notable impacts on

UN peacekeeping missions, affecting their legitimacy and effectiveness.

Misinformation and disinformation campaigns often target the legitimacy of UN missions, contributing to calls for their withdrawal and criticism of their operations. In Mali, contrasting narratives depict the French and Russian missions differently, reflecting broader dissatisfaction and complex local sentiments towards international peacekeeping efforts. These differing portrayals highlight the influence of local perceptions on the effectiveness of peacekeeping missions.

Local perceptions of protection play a crucial role in shaping responses to peacekeeping missions. A recent report on Abyei emphasises the significance of local perceptions in understanding the effectiveness and reception of peacekeeping operations. The perception of protection by local populations directly influences their support or opposition to these missions.

Impact of Misinformation and Disinformation

Misinformation and disinformation are used strategically by various agents and influencers, often mobilising young people to participate in protests and other forms of resistance against peacekeeping missions. In the DRC, slogans like 'MONUSCO (The United Nations Organisation Stabilisation Mission in the Democratic Republic of the Congo) is killed in DRC' and 'MONUSCO in Moscow' reflect deep-seated frustrations and criticisms directed at UN missions, fuelled by false information and negative propaganda. These dynamics underscore the critical challenges posed by MDM to UN peacekeeping missions and their efforts to maintain peace and stability.

Recent observations have highlighted an increase in protests and demonstrations outside UN bases. Interestingly, research reveals that these protests correlate with a significant rise in the authority of mandates, particularly concerning the language used. Despite the increased number and specificity of mandates, the resources allocated to these initiatives often need to be increased. This discrepancy between the mandates and their implementation underscores the need for a more balanced approach.

Response of UN Peacekeeping Operations

UN Peacekeeping Operations (UNPKO) have responded by increasing their presence on social media platforms like Twitter, Instagram, and LinkedIn. These efforts aim to promote training and engage younger influencers to communicate the mission's activities. While this strategy has shown some success, it tends to adopt a more strategic military stance rather than a people-centred approach. This shift results in efforts that are more offensive, rather than understanding and addressing the needs of the local population.

The current force commander's strategies at UN Mission in South Sudan (UNMISS) emphasise engaging with civilians through civil affairs patrols rather than relying solely on traditional radio communication. This approach focuses on the qualitative aspects of patrols, enhancing their interaction with civilians. Consequently, these engagements' success rates are notably higher than those of other missions. However, the challenge remains to maintain a consistent and proactive approach, particularly in politically sensitive times like elections.

Challenges Faced by United Nations Peacekeeping

The vocalisation and politicisation of mission objectives, often through declarations, highlight failures in the PoC, or are politically motivated to divert attention from state responsibilities. This broader condemnation of the mission is frequently employed without considering the consequences or impact on the UNPKO or its staff. Such criticism can be linked to security failures, UN responses to insecurity, or human rights issues, creating unusual links to coping with rebellions and armed conflicts.

These situations often lead to calls for withdrawal or re-evaluation of the mission or its leadership, along with increased criticism of UNPKO for failing to meet high expectations in ending insecurity. Additionally, the rapid spread of misinformation across platforms like TikTok, Twitter, WhatsApp, Signal, and YouTube adds another level of complexity for UNPKO and its civilian dimensions.

One of the most significant challenges UN peacekeeping missions face is the politicisation of elections and specific incidents. When PoC issues arise, missions sometimes appear to remain silent, underscoring the need for more proactive communication to address these challenges effectively. Broader condemnation from the mission can be useful, but more is needed from the civilian perspective. Understanding why civilians protest and addressing their needs more effectively remains crucial. The traditional military-focused approach of UN peacekeeping missions needs to adapt to the rapid dissemination of misinformation, which often leaves missions lagging by several days, hindering their ability to counteract false information and address the resulting challenges.

Recommendations

A comprehensive, people-centred approach should be adopted, integrating strategies to analyse, address, and tackle the embedded use of Misinformation, Disinformation, Malinformation, and Hate speech (MDMH). This approach should be embedded and institutionalised within and beyond mission strategies and coordination structures. Technical, experienced, and trained staff with context-specific knowledge and analytical capacity are essential to monitor and analyse the information environment and identify potential threats.

Enhanced coordination within the mission and with other missions on MDMH issues is necessary. Reporting lines should be integrated into the office of the Special Representative of the Secretary-General (SRSG) or the Deputy SRSG, with focal points at the joint operations centre and joint mission analysis centre. Strategic communication efforts should include the specific contexts and issues covered by the field offices. Stakeholder engagement strategies should employ a whole-of-mission approach, engaging all members of society and considering the impact of social media.

Revised UNPKO mandates should clearly define the link between MDMH threats and PoC, providing clarity on the mission's mandate and necessary steps. Member States, through the Special Committee on Peacekeeping Operations, should request the secretariat to develop indicators of information harms and systematically document the impact of MDMH on safety, security, and mandate implementation. Support and sharing of lessons learned and context-specific best practices on responses to MDMH with UN Headquarters and other struggling missions are essential.

Pre-deployment preparations should include better language training for Troop Contributing Countries to improve their communication and social media presence, aligning it with the mission strategy regarding strategic communication and community protection.

Wider stakeholder engagement is needed to address these issues comprehensively, extending beyond high-level strategic engagement to include everyday people affected by conflict and crisis. Engaging with these individuals provides a deeper understanding of the issues and challenges, crucial for the UN's future operations.

Conclusion

In conclusion, the difficulties presented by MDMH have a big influence on the legitimacy and efficacy of UNPKO. These difficulties heighten hostilities and obstruct initiatives to safeguard civilians and preserve peace. A holistic, people-centred strategy is necessary to address these difficulties. The success of peacekeeping operations can be improved by countering the transmission of false information through the use of context-specific methods, trained staff, enhanced coordination, strategic communication, and stakeholder engagement. To maintain peace and safeguard vulnerable populations, UN peacekeeping tactics must be adjusted to the quickly changing information landscape.

Use of Force for the Protection of Civilians

Major General (Dr) AK Bardalai, VSM (Retd)
Former Deputy Head of the Mission and Deputy Force
Commander, United Nations Interim Force in Lebanon [10]

Introduction

For those missions that are mandated to protect civilians, local perception is a barometer of success. When failure to protect is attributed to the peacekeepers, the trust is lost. Despite the authority vested in the peacekeepers to use force to protect civilians, there are instances of peacekeepers hesitating to use force for protection. On the other hand, there are examples of peacekeepers using force for the Protection of Civilians (PoC), but the civilians continue to suffer. The question, therefore, arises about the utility in using force to protect civilians. The PoC mandate, grounded in international laws, provides legal authority to the peacekeepers. [11] Since there is no peacekeeping force directly under the command of the United Nations (UN), the decision of the UN Security Council (UNSC) and operationalisation of the mandate are hostage to the Troop Contributing Countries (TCCs).

Why do Peacekeepers hesitate to use force?

PoC at cross purposes with the Principles of Peacekeeping.

- The effectiveness of PoC depends on the host state's consent, the first of the three principles of UN peacekeeping.[12] Consent, however, is never absolute, and it comes with conditions. When, for any reason, any of these conditions is diluted, the host state withdraws the consent and stops cooperating in implementing the mandate. To make things worse, when the host state itself is complicit in the crimes against its citizens, and if the strategic interests of the TCCs conflict with the host state, TCCs will be weary of their peacekeepers using force against those who have committed the crime.[13] Soldiers of the South Sudan government stormed Hotel Terrain on 11 Jul 2016 and killed and abused the foreign workers, and the failure of the United Nations Mission in South Sudan (UNMISS) to respond immediately is a glaring example. If they had responded, the South Sudan government would have considered the peacekeepers as partial. However, by not reacting, to the local population, the peacekeepers failed in their duties to protect them.[14]

• The UNSC authorising 'Use of all necessary means', under Chapter VII, has legal implications as it can be interpreted to use even lethal force. Using lethal force may exaggerate violence, reduce the scope of dialogue, encourage peacekeepers to abuse their authority, and increase vulnerability to both peacekeepers and civilians. Besides, practical measures used for protection can be viewed by the different parties as political. The action of the force intervention brigade in 2013 and the UNSC's decision to remove the peacebuilding part of the UNMISS mandate in 2014 because South Sudan not doing enough to protect its civilians in 2013, are two such examples.[15] The PoC mandate, therefore, seems to act at cross purposes with the principles of peacekeeping and leads to a lack of will to use force.

Inadequate Resources. The inadequate number of peacekeepers and wherewithal, which is usually the case, becomes the limiting factor when it comes to using force, even though there is a will to use force for protection.

Ambiguity in Phraseology. There is ambiguity in the interpretation of the use of force. For example, what does the defence of mandate entail? Does it include pre-emptive or offensive measures or is there a limit to escalation? What is the meaning of self-defence and what is the quantum of force that can be considered as a minimum?[16] Such ambiguity becomes a restraining factor for Civilian Police (CIVPOL) as well. For example, 'Using all necessary means' can be confusing if the CIVPOL doesn't have the executive mandate to arrest and detain. When CIVPOL does not disarm the armed militants who threaten civilians because of a lack of executive mandate, to the local population, CIVPOL is reluctant to use force to disarm armed groups.

Knowledge Overload. This is not cited as a reason for not using force. However, too much information such as legal implications can add to the already confused minds, resulting in hesitancy in the use of force.

Ambiguous Protection of Civilians Policy. The latest UN policy of 2023 has re-emphasised the PoC operational concept of three-tier action (Tier I: Protection through dialogue and engagement; Tier II: Provision of physical protection and Tier III: Establishment of a protective environment), which was given in the policy of 2019.[17] Despite being exhaustive, the peacekeepers may understand the norm differently. For instance, one of the guiding principles of the PoC mandate is that the protection of civilians must be fully consonant with the three principles of peacekeeping. But Tier 2 and 3 might involve the use of force. Even the UN's New Agenda for Protection which took years to come out gives out only guidelines. Nothing is mentioned about how to operationalise the PoC mandate.[18]

Protection of Civilians Mandates and Caveats. There are times when the PoC mandate comes with Caveats like, a) focus only on those who are under immediate and direct threat; b) shelter/protect those who are near the bases, it then raises the question how those who don't fall in these categories will be protected?

Protection of Civilians versus Responsibility to Protect. The concepts of PoC and Responsibility to Protect (R2P) are both grounded in the need to protect civilians and are supported by international laws.[19] The main difference is that PoC is a legal concept and on the other hand, R2P is a political principle designed to prevent genocide, war crimes, crimes against humanity and ethnic cleansing. While there are similarities, there are differences. Therefore, PoC and R2P are related, and the relationship is complex, generating controversies with some TCCs maintaining different positions on the subject.[20] A lack of understanding of the difference may create more confusion while operationalising R2P and PoC resulting in ignoring the responsibility to protect the civilians. The variable notion of protection adds to this confusion. Some notions of western militaries using force against those who attack civilians and use force for prevention are linked to R2P. Therefore, conflating R2P and PoC could affect the legal aspects of IHL.

Current Conflicts and Protection

As and when the host states have failed to protect their citizens, which is their responsibility, the UN peace operations did that to the best of their abilities. But as and when the local populations felt they were not safe, even when the peacekeepers were authorised to use force to protect them, cooperation and trust were lost, resulting in countries like Mali and Democratic Republic of Congo (DRC) issuing marching orders to the missions. The question arises of how they would protect their citizens after the exit of the missions. The obvious answer is outsourcing security to external agencies that promise political and diplomatic support to the nations amidst conflicts. It is already happening with the hiring of Private Military Contractors (PMC) or mercenaries. Nigeria's success in fighting Boko Haram in 2015 must be one of the motivating factors amongst others. The mercenaries or the PMCs are for business and, thence, mercenaries love to feast on instability. As long as fighting continues, there will be collateral damage with innocent civilians becoming the prime victims. Who then protects these civilians?

This is not the first time that the UN has faced such a challenge. After the Rwandan genocide, when the Tutsis rebounded and launched a counter-offensive, many genocidal Rwandan soldiers fled and took shelter in the refugee camps in Eastern DRC, one of the options suggested by one Permanent 5 member was to hire PMCs to protect the civilians. It was not agreed to employ PMCs because it would have amounted to the UN abdicating its primary responsibility. The result was the Rwandan Armed Forces took matters into their own hands and hostilities returned to the Rwanda-Zaire (DRC was known as Zaire at that time) border. What is the option then? The new agenda for peace hopefully will find a balance.[21]

Utility of the Use of Force to Protect Civilians

In inter-state conflicts like the Ukraine and Gaza Wars, neither the PoC policy nor the R2P are relevant as these are meant to be applied selectively. In intra-state conflicts, the entry of the PMCs has made protection strategy more challenging.

If the states are committed to security sector reform amid the conflict, there won't be any need to hire PMCs for PoC. Since, security sector reform is a sensitive subject and is seen as intrusive, the international community seems to continue to grapple with the challenges for some time. However, if the PMCs become members of the International Stability Operations Association (ISOA), formerly the International Peace Operations Association, and uphold the ethical standards set out in the ISOA code of conduct, PMCs could be a force multiplier. But the probability of this happening is remote.[22] As for the peacekeepers, regardless of policies and laws, if there is a will, peacekeepers can fulfil their moral obligations to protect. This happened earlier and is happening even now. While there are challenges in using force to protect civilians, there are also instances of commanders using force to protect civilians. In this regard, a few examples are worth looking at.

The first example dates to as early as the 1990s, much before the PoC had become the core objective of the UN. In Srebrenica, in Dec 1993, in several incidents, the contingent forcefully intervened and used force to break through barricades to protect refugees and prevent the cover-up of ethnic cleansing operations by Bosnian Serbs.[23] In another one out of many incidents in South Sudan, when an internal communal clash broke out in Malakal on 18 Feb 2014, Indian peacekeepers, disregarding their safety positioned themselves in between armed groups and prevailed upon to find a solution using means other than violence.[24] Similarly, on 7 Sep 2022, the White Army, one of the local militia groups attacked the IDPs camp on the West bank of the River Nile in the Upper Nile State of South Sudan. The Indian contingent in whose area of operations the IDP camp was located (approximately 150 km from the nearest post of the UNMISS), reacted quickly to deter the armed group from further attacking the camp with orders to use force in self-defence, if necessary.[25]

There must be many more such examples of peacekeepers using force to protect civilians. What comes to light, the cases of failure without reasoning as to why the peacekeepers were unable to protect. The perception about the decreasing utility of using force for protection is because, in the public domain, there are more instances of peacekeepers hesitating to use force as opposed to the instances of peacekeepers standing on the line of fire to save innocent lives.

The search question, however, is how does one apply the IHL on the states that are committing genocide and the state-sponsored mercenaries who are there only for the loot? This will remain a challenge not only to the UN and the member states but also to the countries that are in the midst of armed conflicts.

Challenges in the Application of International Humanitarian Law and Leveraging Modern Technology to Protect Civilians

Gunjan Chawla,
Legal Adviser, International Committee for Red Cross,
Regional Delegation for India, Nepal, Bhutan and the
Maldives

International Committee for Red Cross's Approach to Emerging Technologies

Technological developments have given rise to its inclusion in warfare, such as cyberattacks, drones, robots, creating novel humanitarian and legal challenges. While developing or acquiring new weapons, means or methods of warfare, it is important for a state to assess whether such developments or acquisitions are compliant with the International Humanitarian Law (IHL). Applying pre-existing rules like the Geneva Convention and the Additional Protocols to new technology raises questions with regard to the sufficiency of these laws in light of today's technology's specific characteristics and foreseeable humanitarian impact.[26] Therefore, there arises an urgent need to understand technological developments and their military potential, and assess the potential human cost arising from the increasing use of cyber operations during armed conflicts. Depending on what such assessments point to, work needs to be done on clarification and development of the law.

In this context, two specific aspects of emerging technologies and their interaction with contemporary warfare will be discussed; firstly, Autonomous Weapons Systems (AWS) and secondly, the use of cyber operations in armed conflict. A clear contrast will be noticed in this discussion. Artificial Intelligence and AWS will be discussed first, focusing primarily on how they present challenges in the contemporary IHL norms, and what ICRC recommends in that respect. Then, cyber operations in armed conflict will be discussed, and it will be noticed that solutions to minimising civilian harm comes not just from interpreting and applying the law faithfully, but it must be complemented by the development of a technological solution.

Autonomous Weapons Systems and International Humanitarian Law

AWS systems are weapon systems that, after activation or launch by a person, select and apply force without intervention. There are multiple risks associated with them, because they entail loss of human control and judgement in the use of force, thereby, putting a risk of violation of IHL norms.[27]

For AWS, a short video[28] is presented that encompasses much of the important points on the debate around autonomous weapon systems and how that interact with IHL

Governments have been increasingly spending on autonomous systems and machines that can be remotely operated during warfare. Possibilities of systems that select and attack without human intervention has grown largely. Technologies like submarines, tanks, robots, can be remotely controlled and operated, drones can be interconnected to attack together. Such automated weapons often bear the risk of hitting the wrong target, and even if they hit the right target, the risk to civilians and civilian infrastructure is difficult to gauge and limit. Even though the advent of these newer weapons technologies brought with them the promise of making war more 'humane' by using exquisite precision in targeting for attacks, but this state-of-the-art technology still leaves a significant margin of error. The inability of a weapon system to distinguish between a combatant and a civilian creates a very high, unacceptable level of risk.

The use of autonomous weapons during warfare increases the speed at which weapons are deployed, which in turn increases the risk of attacks going out of human intervention. A weapon system capable of selecting targets on its own, without human intervention will be unable to make decisions that are comparable with human judgment in their ability to comply with the principles of distinction, proportionality, and precautions as well as the IHL prohibitions on indiscriminate attacks. By using AWS, not only is human dignity being undermined by those who suffer the consequences of life-or-death decisions being made by programmable machine, but the decision to deploy such systems also undermines the human agency of those on the attacking side. The AWS' inability to comply with essential rules and the IHL principles in the conduct of hostilities raises serious questions as to their legality in the current regime.

International Committee for Red Cross's position

In how IHL interacts with the advent of AWS, the ICRC takes the view that there is an urgent need to negotiate a new legally binding instrument to ban certain kinds of AWS, namely, anti-personnel AWS and unpredictable AWS.[28] For other types of AWS, their use ought to be regulated by restricting to certain identified circumstances. There is a need to place limitations on the types of targets, duration, geographical scope and scale of use, limits on situations of use of AWS in addition to creating requirements for human-machine interaction. That is to say, the new legally binding instrument would outlaw the use of certain kinds of AWS and regulate the use of others. It is important to flag at this stage, that when the ICRC recommends a new treaty – or an amendment to the law as it stands today, it does not do so lightly, but with the full awareness that the replication of a universal consensus on an IHL treaty that was seen for the GC 75 years ago is an extremely challenging endeavour, but is made necessary by the greatly troubling impact of the deployment of such technologies on the civilian population.[29]

This approach of developing legal solutions can be easily contrasted with the approach taken in the context of the use of cyber operations in armed conflict.

Cyber Operations in the Armed Conflicts

In the past two to three decades, the proliferation of cyber operations, especially against critical infrastructures such as petrochemical plants, power grids, nuclear facilities, hospitals and other healthcare facilities has a direct adverse impact on the lives of civilians and their survivability, especially when such operations are orchestrated in the context of an armed conflict.

From an IHL standpoint, the same rules on conduct of hostilities discussed in the context of AWS become relevant and applicable to cyber operations in armed conflict – the prohibition on indiscriminate attacks, as well as the requirements to adhere to the principles of distinction, proportionality and precautions remain crucial to conduct these cyber operations lawfully. After some initial doubts, it is now amply clear and well accepted that IHL applies to cyber operations in armed conflict even if disagreements remain as to exactly how the IHL applies to such military activity.

The relevance of the IHL to cyber operations cannot be understated. As societies digitalise, cyber operations are becoming a reality of armed conflict. The number of States developing military cyber capabilities continues to grow, and it is expected that the use of these capabilities during armed conflict will increase. Cyber operations have become an established feature of military operations today. Indeed, IHL applies to cyber operations in armed conflict, but its application still requires a great deal of operationalisation. Precautions remain a key method to avoiding civilian harm, especially with respect to the protection of healthcare facilities, the attacking side must verify whether the object or facility being subjected to attack is entitled to legal protections from attack under IHL. While in some cases, the deployment of cyber operations may allow militaries to achieve their objectives with relatively less destruction, their use against healthcare facilities in particular could have devastating consequences for the protection of civilian lives and dignity.

Digitalisation of the Distinctive Emblems

In this pursuit, the ICRC is currently exploring certain technological solutions that hold the potential to operationalise legal protections for medical and humanitarian facilities and personnel from attacks. This is a project that has been developed in partnership with the Johns Hopkins University Applied Physics Laboratory and the Centre for Cyber Trust (Which is a joint endeavour of the Eidgenössische Technische Hochschule Zurich and the

University of Bonn) and the Australian Red Cross. A detailed report on the specifications of the project was published in late 2022.[30]

Just as the distinctive Red Cross, Red Crescent and Red Crystal emblems have for decades signaled these legal protections in the physical realm,[31] the Authenticated Digital Emblem seeks to make analogous protections perceptible and legible to operators in cyberspace. The digitalised avatar of the distinctive emblem was a project initiated by the ICRC a few years ago, and is now in the stage of wider consultations being conducted with the partners in the Red Cross and Red Crescent movement as well as state governments and the private sector to assess the feasibility of its deployment with a view to leveraging the protective power of the distinctive emblem in cyberspace.

The main benefit expected from a digital emblem is that it would make it easier for those conducting cyber operations (hereafter called 'Cyber Operators') to identify and spare protected entities by visualising and operationalising legal protections in the Information and Communication Technologies environment. In the 'Fog of War', this additional signal can have real added value. It will primarily enhance protection for marked entities against the risk of harm caused by law-abiding operators; however, it may also have a deterrent effect on malicious ones. A digital emblem signals legal protection under the IHL norms, and cannot be expected to replace defensive measures against harmful cyber operations. For the protection against cyber operations, cyber-security measures still have to be implemented by protected entity. Additionally, once developed, digital emblems would need to be easy to deploy, remove, and maintainable at a low cost, along with being easily identifiable.

Thus, this new piece of technology which is being developed through a collaborative approach, holds the potential to greatly minimise risks for civilians and healthcare facilities, as well as humanitarian organisations from cyber operations.

Conclusion

In conclusion, the advent of new technologies, specifically AWS, entails the assessment of existing laws and finding out whether they sufficiently cover the characteristics and humanitarian impacts of AWS. ICRC advocates for a new legally binding instrument to prohibit specific types of AWS, namely unpredictable weapons and weapons that target civilians and protected persons, and strictly regulate the usage of all other weapon systems.

On the other hand, ICRC's position with respect to cyber operations leads to the conclusion that the effective protection of civilians in contemporary and future conflicts requires not just application and operationalisation of existing IHL, but also the development and implementation of new legal tools and technological solutions.

Adherence to International Humanitarian Law by State and Non-State Actors

Kasim Balarabe
Professor and Associate Dean, O P Jindal Global
University

Introduction

The International Humanitarian Law (IHL), also known as the law of armed conflict or the law of war, is a set of rules that aim to limit the effects of armed conflict on civilians, combatants, and those no longer participating in hostilities. The origins of the IHL can be traced back to the 19th century, with the adoption of the first Geneva Convention (GC) in 1864.[32] The four GC of 1949 and their Additional Protocols (APs) form the core of IHL, establishing detailed rules for the treatment of wounded and sick soldiers, prisoners of war, and civilians in armed conflict.[33] These instruments also define the rights and obligations of parties to a conflict, including the principles of distinction, proportionality, and precaution in the conduct of hostilities. In addition to the GCs, Customary International Humanitarian Law (CIHL) plays a significant role in regulating the behaviour of parties in armed conflicts, referring to the unwritten rules that have emerged from the consistent practice of states and their belief in the binding nature of these rules.[34]

The International Committee for Red Cross (ICRC) is a key factor in developing and promoting the IHL, working as an impartial, neutral, and independent organisation to ensure respect for IHL by all parties to armed conflicts.[35] However, the adherence to the IHL by non-state actors remains a significant challenge in today's complex landscape of armed conflicts. States, as the primary actors bound by the IHL, have a legal and moral obligation to respect and ensure respect for these rules, but political and military considerations and the lack of effective enforcement mechanisms have often led to non-adherence.[36] Non-state actors, such as armed opposition groups and rebel forces, pose an additional challenge to the adherence to the IHL due to their need for recognition and legitimacy, combined with their often limited awareness of the IHL principles.[37] The consequences of non-adherence to the IHL are devastating, with civilians bearing the brunt of these violations, countless lives lost, communities displaced, and infrastructure destroyed.[38]

International Humanitarian Law Adherence by Non-State Actors

The Applicability of International Humanitarian Law to Non-State Actors.

• The IHL applies not only to states but also to non-state actors involved in armed conflicts. The GCs, their APs, and CIHL provide a legal framework that binds all parties to an armed conflict, including non-state armed groups.

• Common Article 3 of the GCs, which applies to non-international armed conflicts, expressly mentions 'Each Party to the Conflict', indicating that its provisions also bind non-state armed groups.[39] These provisions include the prohibition of violence against persons not taking an active part in hostilities, the requirement to treat the wounded and sick humanely, and the prohibition of outrages upon personal dignity. AP II, which develops and supplements Common Article 3, applies to non-international armed conflicts between state armed forces and dissident armed forces or other organised armed groups.[40] It sets out more detailed rules on the protection of civilians, the treatment of persons whose liberty has been restricted, and the conduct of hostilities.[41]

• CIHL, which consists of rules derived from state practice and *opinio juris* (Opinion of Law), also applies to non-state armed groups.[42] The ICRC's study on customary IHL identified 161 rules, many of which are applicable in both international and non-international armed conflicts. These rules cover various aspects of IHL, including the principle of distinction, the prohibition of indiscriminate attacks, and the protection of civilians and persons *hors de combat* (Temporarily out of Combat).[43]

• The applicability of the IHL to non-state actors is based on the principle of equality of belligerents, which holds that the rights and obligations under IHL apply equally to all parties to an armed conflict, regardless of the legitimacy of their cause.[44]

Challenges in Ensuring Non-State Actor Compliance with International Humanitarian Law.

• Despite the applicability of the IHL to non-state actors, ensuring their compliance with these rules remains a significant challenge. The lack of recognition and legitimacy under international law, the absence of formal training and awareness, and ideological and strategic considerations contribute to the difficulties in holding non-state armed groups accountable for IHL violations.

• The lack of recognition and legitimacy of non-state armed groups can make it difficult for them to engage with international organisations and Non-Governmental Organisations (NGOs) that promote the IHL compliance. The absence of formal training and awareness among these groups can lead to a poor understanding of IHL principles and rules, increasing the likelihood of violations.[45] The possible absence of a clear command structure and internal disciplinary mechanisms within some non-state armed groups can also hinder the enforcement of IHL.[46]

• Ideological and strategic considerations can also pose significant challenges to non-state actor compliance with IHL. Some non-state armed groups may have ideologies that are incompatible with the principles of IHL, such as the rejection of the distinction between civilians and combatants.[47] Strategic considerations, such as the power asymmetry between non-state armed groups and state armed forces, can also contribute to IHL violations, as non-state actors may resort to tactics that violate IHL as a means of compensating for their military weakness.

Consequences of Non-State Actors' Non-Adherence to International Humanitarian Law.

• The consequences of non-state actors' non-adherence to the IHL are severe and far-reaching. Violations of the IHL, such as the deliberate targeting of civilians, the use of indiscriminate weapons, and the denial of humanitarian assistance, can result in widespread death, injury, and displacement, often disproportionately affecting vulnerable groups.

• Non-state actors' non-adherence to the IHL can prolong armed conflicts and hinder efforts to achieve sustainable peace by leading to cycles of violence and retaliation.[48] It can also undermine the credibility and legitimacy of these groups, eroding their support among the local population and leading to international condemnation and sanctions.[49]

• Non-adherence to the IHL by non-state actors can have long-term consequences for post-conflict reconciliation and transitional justice, creating a legacy of trauma and resentment that can persist long after the end of hostilities and making it more challenging to achieve accountability for past abuses and promote healing among affected communities.

Strategies for Enhancing Adherence to International Humanitarian Law
Strengthening Legal Frameworks and Enforcement Mechanisms.

• This is crucial for enhancing adherence to the IHL. One strategy is to encourage more states to ratify and implement the APs, which provide detailed rules for protecting civilians and conducting hostilities. Another approach is to promote the adoption of new legal instruments to address emerging challenges, such as the use of autonomous weapons systems or the protection of the environment during warfare.

• Reinforcing the role of international criminal tribunals, such as the International Criminal Court (ICC), in prosecuting serious violations of the IHL is also essential. This can be achieved by encouraging more states to ratify the Rome Statute, providing adequate resources to the ICC, and promoting cooperation between the ICC and national jurisdictions.[50] Strengthening the capacity of national courts to investigate and prosecute IHL violations through the application of universal jurisdiction can also help close the impunity gap and deter future violations.[51]

Promoting International Humanitarian Law Education and Awareness Among State and Non-State Actors. Promoting IHL education and awareness among non-state actors is another critical strategy. Engaging with non-state armed groups to provide IHL training and disseminate information can increase their understanding and acceptance of IHL principles.[52] Civil society organisations and academic institutions also play a vital role in raising public awareness and providing training and capacity-building support.

Engaging with Non-State Actors to Encourage Compliance. Engaging with non-state actors to encourage compliance with the IHL is crucial for reducing the impact of armed conflicts on civilian populations. Dialogue and persuasion can be used to build trust and understanding and to persuade groups to respect the IHL.[53] Incentives and disincentives, such as access to humanitarian aid or the threat of sanctions, can also be used to encourage compliance. Supporting the capacity of non-state actors to implement the IHL through technical assistance and resources can help them develop internal codes of conduct, disciplinary procedures, and training programmes.

Leveraging Technology to Monitor and Report International Humanitarian Law Violations. Leveraging technology to monitor and report the IHL violations is an emerging strategy for enhancing adherence to the IHL. Satellite imagery can be used to detect and report attacks on civilian objects, while social media and online platforms can be used to collect and verify information on IHL violations.[54] Mobile phone applications and messaging platforms can also facilitate the reporting of IHL violations by civilians and combatants. However, the use of technology for monitoring and reporting also raises challenges, such as the protection of privacy and the security of those reporting abuses and the need to ensure the credibility and reliability of the information collected.

Enhancing Accountability and Prosecution of IHL Violations. Enhancing accountability and prosecution of IHL violations is critical for ensuring adherence to the IHL and deterring future abuses. Strengthening the capacity of national courts to investigate and prosecute the IHL violations through training, resources, and the adoption of legislation incorporating the IHL into domestic law is one approach.[55] Supporting the work of international criminal tribunals, such as the ICC, through political and financial support and cooperation with investigations and arrest warrants is another. Addressing the challenges of gathering evidence in conflict zones and protecting witnesses and victims through the support of international fact-finding missions and the establishment of witness protection programmes is also essential. In addition to criminal prosecutions, other accountability mechanisms, such as truth and reconciliation commissions, reparations programmes, and institutional reforms, can help address the root causes of conflict and promote healing and reconciliation.

The Role of the International Community

Diplomatic Efforts to Promote Adherence to International Humanitarian Law. Diplomatic efforts by state and non-state actors are crucial in promoting adherence to the IHL. These efforts can take various forms, such as bilateral and multilateral engagements, public statements, and international forums to address IHL-related issues. For example, the regular meetings of the High Contracting Parties to the GCs allow states to reaffirm their commitment to the IHL, share best practices, and address challenges in implementing the law.[56] Diplomatic efforts can also involve using demarches and formal diplomatic communications to convey specific messages or requests to another state, expressing concern about the IHL violations, calling for investigations and accountability, and urging compliance with particular provisions of the law. Multilateral forums, such as the United Nations Security Council and the Human Rights Council, can adopt resolutions, issue statements, and establish fact-finding missions or commissions of inquiry to address IHL related issues. Diplomatic efforts can also be directed towards non-state armed groups, encouraging them to respect IHL and engage in dialogue on compliance, often involving intermediaries such as NGOs or religious leaders.

Providing Support and Resources for International Humanitarian Law Implementation. Providing support and resources for the IHL implementation is another crucial aspect. This can involve financial assistance, technical expertise, and capacity-building initiatives to help states and other actors fulfil their obligations under the IHL. The ICRC is a key example of an organisation that provides a wide range of services to victims of armed conflict, promotes respect for the IHL, and monitors compliance. The international community can also provide financial support for IHL-related initiatives, such as establishing national IHL committees, translating and disseminating the IHL treaties and materials, and organising training and awareness-raising activities. Additionally, the international community can encourage and facilitate the sharing of best practices and lessons learned in the IHL implementation through conferences, workshops, and other forums for exchange and dialogue.

Strengthening the Capacity of International Organisations and Non-Governmental Organisations. International organisations and NGOs play a critical role in promoting adherence to the IHL and monitoring and reporting compliance. Strengthening these actors' capacity is essential to the international community's efforts to enhance IHL implementation. The United Nations (UN), through its various agencies and bodies, regularly addresses IHL related issues and adopts resolutions and statements on compliance. To strengthen the UN's capacity to fulfil its IHL-related mandate, the international community can provide political and financial support, as well as expertise and resources. NGOs, such as Human Rights Watch and Amnesty International investigate and report on IHL violations, assist victims, and advocate for accountability and compliance. To strengthen the capacity of NGOs, the international community can provide financial and technical support, as well as protection and access, including funding for investigations, reporting, and advocacy activities, and providing training and resources on the IHL and human rights monitoring.

Encouraging Public Awareness and Advocacy for International Humanitarian Law Adherence. Encouraging public awareness and advocacy for IHL adherence is another crucial aspect of the international community's role in promoting compliance with the law. The media plays a significant role in informing the public about the IHL and highlighting violations and abuses, and the international community can support their work by providing training and resources on the IHL and reporting in conflict situations. Civil society organisations and movements can help mobilise public opinion and pressure governments and other actors to respect the IHL and take action to prevent and punish violations. The international community can offer access, protection, and financial and technical support to civil society groups and movements to foster and promote IHL compliance, including funding for public campaigns, research, and advocacy activities, and providing training and resources on the IHL and human rights.

Conclusion

Enhancing adherence to the IHL by non-state actors is crucial for protecting civilians and regulating armed conflicts in the contemporary world. While the IHL applies to all parties to an armed conflict, including non-state armed groups, ensuring their compliance remains a significant challenge due to various factors such as lack of recognition, absence of formal training, and ideological and strategic considerations. The consequences of non-adherence to the IHL by non-state actors are severe, leading to widespread suffering, prolonged conflicts, and hindered efforts towards sustainable peace.

To address these challenges, a multifaceted approach is necessary. Strengthening international legal frameworks and enforcement mechanisms, promoting IHL education and awareness, engaging with non-state actors through dialogue and incentives, leveraging technology for monitoring and reporting violations, and enhancing accountability and prosecution are key strategies that can contribute to improved IHL adherence. The international community plays a vital role in these efforts through diplomatic initiatives, providing support and resources, strengthening the capacity of relevant organisations, and encouraging public awareness and advocacy.

By implementing these strategies and fostering a global commitment to the IHL, the international community can work towards enhancing the protection of civilians, mitigating the devastating consequences of armed conflicts, and promoting a culture of respect for the IHL among all parties to armed conflicts, including non-state actors.

82

Closing Session

Major General PK Goswami, VSM (Retd)
Deputy Director General and Head UN Centre, USI

Protection of Civilians (PoC) in modern conflicts and International Humanitarian Law (IHL) has been repeatedly highlighted in various international forums, like G-20 New Delhi Leaders Declaration, on 09 Sep 2023, which called for 'All states to uphold the principles of International Humanitarian Law'. Similarly, on 31 Oct 2023, United Nations Secretary-General Antonio Guterres, in a statement on the situation in Gaza, said "IHL establishes clear rules that cannot be ignored. It is not a la carte menu and cannot be applied selectively. All parties must abide by it, including the principles of distinction, proportionality and precaution". However, despite all efforts, emerging threats of new technologies, misinformation and disinformation, and the presence of non-state actors, including private military and security companies, have changed the way armed conflict is fought with non-adherence to IHL principles; resulting in continued risks to civilians in the conflict zone.

Today modern conflicts are being triggered by three fundamental challenges - The first is the very tense state of major power relations, which is clearly doing great harm to humanity and the United Nations Security Council (UNSC). Secondly, there is a lack of trust between developed countries and developing nations – Global North and Global South. Finally, today United Nations (UN) seems to be just not very relevant or well calibrated to deal with some of the big contemporary issues. The UN system is designed to fix the problems of the 1960s, thus, affects its capacity to deal with the prevailing global conflict environment. Resulting in powerful states adopting their own line of action, and non-compliance of the rule of law.

In fact, humanity today is standing at the threshold, witnessing a deliberate undermining of the collective commitments established to limit the barbarity of war, combined with a lack of accountability when international laws and standards are disregarded. If this accountability gap is not addressed urgently, there is a risk of barrelling further down a path of no return. While the full protection of civilians remains a distant goal, but still it is the one to which all efforts must be directed. Thus, despite the challenges, finding ways to protect civilians from the effects of armed conflict has never been more urgent and relevant.

To sum up, quoting, Ms Mirjana Spoljaric Egger, President, International Committee for Red Cross (ICRC), who while speaking at the Graduate Institute in Geneva on 'International Humanitarian Law in a Divided World' in Nov 2022, said "Among the many challenges confronting IHL today, non-compliance is the most critical".

Thus, the need is to inject renewed urgency into ensuring the implementation of international laws and standards, and UNSC Resolutions, for the protection of civilians in armed conflict. This should include:

- Ensuring IHL, International Human Rights Law (IHRL) and PoC are prioritised as core tenets of global multilateral governance in the forthcoming 'Pact for the Future'.

• Strengthening and implementing legal accountability mechanisms and other safeguards around the use of new technologies in armed conflict.

• A treaty to prohibit and regulate autonomous weapons systems by 2026 as recommended by the UNSG in the New Agenda for Peace.

• Strengthening and implementing international, regional and national legal and regulatory frameworks governing private military and security companies, including mechanisms for transparency, oversight, accountability and redress for civilian harm.

• Establishing an environment, peace, and security agenda to better protect civilians from conflict-linked environmental harm and the impacts of the environment-climate-conflict nexus.

Thus, to address the challenges posed by modern warfare, efforts must be made to adapt and strengthen the IHL and leveraging technology for effective adoption and implementation. But more important is commitment of all member states, as well as the support of the international community.

About the Participants

Major General BK Sharma, AVSM, SM (Retd)** is the Director General, USI, India's oldest think tank established in 1870. He represented his country at the UN as a Military Observer in Central America and has been India's Defence Attaché in Central Asia. He was Senior Faculty Member at the National Defence College, New Delhi.

Mr Kedir Awol Omar, Head of Regional Delegation of the ICRC for India, Nepal, Bhutan and the Maldives. He has decades of operational and regional experience in humanitarian response. He has led various global delegations, ranging from those in conflict settings to humanitarian diplomacy such as Yemen, Sierra Leone, Gaza, Nigeria, Iran, South Africa, Saudi Arabia, Sudan and Kuwait.

Lieutenant General Rakesh Kapoor, AVSM, VSM, Deputy Chief of Army Staff (Information Systems and Coordination), a graduate of US Army War College and former advisor to Botswana Defence Force, the general officer held varied staff, command and instructional appointments and has rich operational experience. He has commanded a Corps in the desert sector before assuming the present appointment last year.

Major General PK Goswami, VSM (Retd), is Deputy Director General and Head UN Cell, USI. He was Military Observer with United Nations Verification Mission at Angola (UNAVEM) and senior faculty at National Defence College, New Delhi. He represented National Defence College at the 16th Association of Southeast Asian Nations Regional Forum for Heads of Defence Universities, Colleges and Institutions at Beijing, China in Nov 2012.

Lieutenant General JS Lidder, UYSM, AVSM (Retd) an Indian Army veteran, with vast UN experience in both political and military spheres. He was Chief of Staff in ONUMOZ (Mozambique) 1994-95 and Force Commander UNMIS (Sudan) from 2005 to 08. Post military retirement, he was Deputy SRSG UNMIS from 2010 to 11. Presently, he is involved with multiple UN Offices, global think tanks, and training establishments as an expert and mentor.

Dr Ajai Sahni, Executive Director, the Institute for Conflict Management, which maintains the South Asia Terrorism Portal, and an author on counter-terrorism

Lieutenant General S Mohan, AVSM, SM, VSM, a serving General officer of Indian Army. He was Defence Attache at Vietnam, Laos and Cambodia; and member of the UN mission at Sierra Leone. He is presently Force Commander, UNMISS (South Sudan).

Major General (Dr) AK Bardalai, VSM (Retd), an Indian Army Veteran, with vast UN experience. He was a Military Observer in the United Nations Verification Mission in Angola in 1991-92 and Deputy Head of the Mission and Deputy Force Commander of United Nations Interim Forces in Lebanon (UNIFIL) from 2008 to 2010. Recently, he teamed up with Geneva Centre for Security Policy and Effectiveness of Peace Operations Network for a study on UN Truce Supervision Organisation and presented it to UN HQ on 31 May 2024.

Dr George Devaladze, Regional Legal Advisor for South Asia, ICRC, New Delhi. He was earlier at the Law and Policy Department of the ICRC, Geneva. His is doctorate in international law from the University of Geneva.

Ms Gunjan Chawla, Legal Advisor, ICRC; in the past has worked at the International Court of Justice, Hague.

Dr Andrew E. Yaw Tchie, Senior Research Fellow, NUPI (Norwegian Institute of International Affairs); an African Expert and Adviser and Visiting Professor University of Buckingham, King's College London. Recently, along with Dr Lotte, he concluded and presented report on Misinformation, Disinformation, Malinformation and hate speech in the digital era.

Professor Dr Kasim Balarabe, a law professor, PhD in Law from Maastricht University, Netherlands, an LLM from Amsterdam and Geneva, with over 17 years of experience. His areas of expertise include public international law, international human rights law, international humanitarian law, international criminal law, international refugee law, and international peace and security issues. Presently, he is Dean with OP Jindal University.

Endnotes

1   Conceptualizing IHL: Denial of Quarter written by Sindija Beta and Dr. Greg Noone - https://www.publicinternationallawandpolicygroup.org/pilpg-ukraine-legal-blog; Other opinions and analysis by Public International Law & Policy Group (PILPG) - https://ccl.org.ua/en/positions/conceptualizing-ihl-denial-of-quarter/; Humar Rights Sit-Rep by the OHCHR - https://www.ohchr.org/sites/default/files/documents/countries/ukraine/2023/23-03-24-Ukraine-35th-periodic-report-ENG.pdf

2   Private Military Contractors (PMCs): https://www.icrc.org/en/download/file/135841/montreux_document_en.pdf;

3   https://www.icrc.org/en/doc/assets/files/other/law1_final.pdf

4   Oberleitner, Gerd. "Human Security: A Challenge to International Law?" Global Governance 11, no. 2 (2005): 185–203. http://www.jstor.org/stable/27800564.

5   https://www.icrc.org/en/document/icrc-report-ihl-and-challenges-contemporary-armed-conflicts

6   https://www.youtube.com/watch?v=iXO2Wv2WpDg

7   https://www.icrc.org/en/publication/4701-war-cities-preventing-and-addressing-humanitarian-consequences-civilians

8   https://www.icrc.org/en/download/file/229018/ewipa_explosive_weapons_with_wide_area_effect_final.pdf

9   https://www.dfa.ie/media/dfa/ourrolepolicies/peaceandsecurity/ewipa/EWIPA-Political-Declaration-Final-Rev-25052022.pdf

10 Major General AK Bardalai (retd) is a former peacekeeper and currently a Distinguished Fellow of the United Services Institute of India. He holds a PhD in UN Peace Operations under the supervision of Prof. Dr. Joseph Soeters, Tilburg University, the Netherlands, and Prof. Dr. Patricia M Shields, Texas State University.

11 "Policy: The Protection of Civilians in United Nations Peacekeeping," UN Department of Peace Operations, Ref.2023.05, May 1, 2023.

12 United Nations Peacekeeping Operations: Principles and Guidelines (New York: UN Department of Peacekeeping Operations, 2008), pp. 31.

13 "Host-Country Consent in UN Peacekeeping: Bridging the Gap between Principle and Practice," Peacekeeping, Stimson, September 8, 2022, https://www.stimson.org/2022/host-country-consent-in-un-peacekeeping-bridging-the-gap-between-principle-and-practice/. Also see, Anjali Dayal, "A Crisis of Consent in UN Peace Operations," IPI Global Observatory, August 2, 2022, https://theglobalobservatory.org/2022/08/a-crisis-of-consent-in-un-peace-operations/

14 Lauren Spink and Matt Wells, "Under Fire: The July 2016 Violence in Juba and UN Response," *Centre for Civilians in Conflict*, October 5, 2016, https://civiliansinconflict.org/publications/research/fire-july-2016-violence-juba-un-response; " UN: Rape used as a tool for ethnic cleansing in South Sudan," *CBS News,* December 2, 2016, https://www.cbsnews.com/news/united-nations-says-rape-used-as-tool-for-ethnic-cleansing-in-south-sudan/

15 Marion Laurence, 'An 'Impartial' Force? Normative Ambiguity and Practice Change in UN Peace operations,' *International Peacekeeping*, 26, no.3 (January 2019), pp. 256-280, DOI:10.108 0/13533312.2018.1517027; UN Security Council Resolution, S/RES2198 March 28, 2013, and S/RES/2277 March 30, 2016.

16 A K Bardalai, "UN Peacekeeping and Ambiguity in Normative UN Norms*," Manohar Parrikar Institute for Defence Studies and Analyses Journal of Defence Studies*, Vol. 16, No. 3, July–September 2022, pp. 3–31. Also see, Rupert Smith, "Bosnia, Using Force Amongst the People," The Utility of Force: The Art of War in the Modern World (England: Penguin, 2005)

17 "Policy: The Protection of Civilians in United Nations Peacekeeping," UN Department of Peace Operations, Ref.2023.05, May 1, 2023. Also see, "The Protection of Civilians in United Nations Peacekeeping", *The UN Department of Peace Operations,* Ref. 2019.17. November 1, 2019

18 Damian Lilly and Jennifer Welsh, "The UN's New Agenda for Protection: Can It Make a Difference?" *IPI Global Observatory,* May 13, 2024, The UN's New Agenda for Protection: Can It Make a Difference? | IPI Global Observatory (theglobalobservatory.org)

19 "Policy: The Protection of Civilians in United Nations Peacekeeping," UN Department of Peace Operations, Ref.2023.05, May 1, 2023.

20 Paul D. Williams, "The R2P, Protection of Civilians, and UN Peacekeeping Operations," Alex J. Bellamy and Tim Dunne, eds *The Oxford Handbook of the Responsibility to Protect* (Oxford University Press, 2016), pp. 524-544

21 UN Security Council, S/RES/2719 (2023) December 21, 2023. Also see, Eugene Chen, "Unpacking Security Council Resolution 2719 (2023)," *New York University Centre on International Cooperation,* February 2024, https://cic.nyu.edu/resources/next-steps-on-the-financing-of-african-peace-support-operations/

22 For more on ISOA, see https://stability-operations.org/.

23 Tony Ingesson, *The Politics of Combat: The Political and Strategic Impact of Tactical Level Sub-Cultures, 1939-1995* (Sweden: Media-Tryck, Lund University, 2026), 235-55

24 As learned from the peacekeeping contingent returned after the end of the tour of duty in South Sudan.

25 Interview with one military staff officer who served as an operational officer in UNMISS at the time of the incident.

26 ICRC, 'ICRC President: We must adopt a human centered approach to the development and use of new technologies' (1 June 2024) https://www.icrc.org/en/war-and-law/weapons/ihl-and-new-technologies accessed 12 June 2024.

27 ICRC's submission on autonomous weapon systems to the United Nations Secretary-General (RE: ODA-2024-00019/LAWS) accessible at <https://www.icrc.org/sites/default/files/wysiwyg/war-and-law/icrc_submission_on_autonomous_weapons_to_unsg.pdf> at p. 4.

28 ICRC position paper on autonomous weapon systems, May 2021, available at: https://www.icrc.org/en/document/icrc-position-autonomous-weapon-systems.

29 Ibid.

30 ICRC's report on Digitalizing the Red Cross, Red Crescent and Red Crystal Emblems: Benefits, Risks, and Possible Solutions, November 2022, available at: https://www.icrc.org/en/document/icrc-digital-emblems-report?mc_phishing_protection_id=28048-cjadlt70s0v8umr75u30.

31 First Geneva Convention, Art. 38-44; Second Geneva Convention, Art. 41; Additional Protocol I, Arts. 8, 18, & 38; Additional Protocol II, Art. 12.

32 François Bugnion, 'The International Committee of the Red Cross and the Development of International Humanitarian Law' (2004) 5(1) Chicago Journal of International Law 191, 191-193.

33 Geneva Convention for the Amelioration of the Condition of the Wounded and Sick in Armed Forces in the Field (adopted 12 August 1949, entered into force 21 October 1950) 75 UNTS 31 (Geneva Convention I); Geneva Convention for the Amelioration of the Condition of Wounded, Sick and Shipwrecked Members of Armed Forces at Sea (adopted 12 August 1949, entered into force 21 October 1950) 75 UNTS 85 (Geneva Convention II); Geneva Convention Relative to the Treatment of Prisoners of War (adopted 12 August 1949, entered into force 21 October 1950) 75 UNTS 135 (Geneva Convention III); Geneva Convention Relative to the Protection of Civilian Persons in Time of War (adopted 12 August 1949, entered into force 21 October 1950) 75 UNTS 287 (Geneva Convention IV). Protocol Additional to the Geneva Conventions of 12 August 1949, and relating to the Protection of Victims of International Armed Conflicts (adopted 8 June 1977, entered into force 7 December 1978) 1125 UNTS 3 (Additional Protocol I); Protocol Additional to the Geneva Conventions of 12 August 1949, and relating to the Protection of Victims of Non-International Armed Conflicts (adopted 8 June 1977, entered into force 7 December 1978) 1125 UNTS 609 (Additional Protocol II).

34 Jean-Marie Henckaerts and Louise Doswald-Beck, *Customary International Humanitarian Law, Volume I: Rules* (Cambridge University Press 2005).

35 See International Committee of the Red Cross, 'International Humanitarian Law and the Challenges of Contemporary Armed Conflicts: Recommitting to Protection in Armed Conflict on the 70th Anniversary of the Geneva Conventions: Document Prepared by the International Committee of the Red Cross for the 33rd International Conference of the Red Cross and Red Crescent, Geneva, Switzerland, 9–12 December 2019' (2019) 101(911) International Review of the Red Cross 869.

36 See Marco Sassòli, 'The Implementation of International Humanitarian Law: Current and Inherent Challenges' (2007) 10

Yearbook of International Humanitarian Law 45. See also Robert Kolb, 'Military Objectives in International Humanitarian Law' (2015) 28(3) Leiden Journal of International Law 691.

37   See Sandesh Sivakumaran, 'Binding Armed Opposition Groups' (2006) 55(2) The International and Comparative Law Quarterly 369. See also Ezequiel Heffes, *Compliance with IHL by Non-State Armed Groups: Some Practical Reflections at the 70th Anniversary of the 1949 Geneva Conventions* (EJIL 21 August 2019).

38   See International Committee of the Red Cross, 'International Humanitarian Law and the Challenges of Contemporary Armed Conflicts: Recommitting to Protection in Armed Conflict on the 70th Anniversary of the Geneva Conventions: Document Prepared by the International Committee of the Red Cross for the 33rd International Conference of the Red Cross and Red Crescent, Geneva, Switzerland, 9–12 December 2019' (2019) 101(911) International Review of the Red Cross 869.

39   Geneva Conventions (n 2) art 3.

40   Additional Protocol II (n 2) art 1.

41   ibid arts 4, 5, 13.

42   See Henckaerts and Doswald-Beck (n 3); Daragh Murray, 'How International Humanitarian Law Treaties Bind Non-State Armed Groups' (2015) 20(1) Journal of Conflict & Security Law 101, 105; Zhuo Liang, 'The Practice of Non-state Armed Groups and the Formation of Customary International Humanitarian Law: Towards Direct Relevance?' in Panos Merkouris, Jörg Kammerhofer and Noora Arajärvi (eds), *The Theory, Practice, and Interpretation of Customary International Law* (The Rules of Interpretation of Customary International Law, Cambridge University Press 2022).

43   Henckaerts and Doswald-Beck (n 3).

44   Jann K. Kleffner, 'The Unilateralization of International Humanitarian Law' (2022) 104(920-921) International Review of the Red Cross 2153, 2159.

45   Hyeran Jo, 'Compliance with International Humanitarian Law by Non-State Armed Groups: How Can It Be Improved?' in Terry D. Gill and others (eds), *Yearbook of International Humanitarian Law Volume 19, 2016* (T.M.C. Asser Press 2018).

46 Daragh Murray, 'Organizing Rebellion: Non-State Armed Groups under International Humanitarian Law, Human Rights Law, and International Criminal Law' (2019) 101(910) International Review of the Red Cross 377; Tilman Rodenhäuser, 'Organized Armed Groups in Contemporary International Practice' in Tilman Rodenhäuser (ed), *Organizing Rebellion: Non-State Armed Groups under International Humanitarian Law, Human Rights Law, and International Criminal Law* (Oxford University Press 2018); Liang (n 11).

47 Sassòli (n 5) 59.

48 Ibid 72.

49 ICRC, 'Protection of Victims of Armed Conflict Through Respect of International Humanitarian Law' (*International Committee of the Red Cross,* 16 September 1999) <https://www.icrc.org/en/doc/resources/documents/misc/57jpzn.htm> accessed 2 June 2024; Emily Daglish, 'Sanctioning Non-State Armed Groups: Does it work?' (*HS Centre,* 14 October 2014) <http://www.hscentre.org/wp-content/uploads/2014/10/PB.-2014.-V10.-N1.-Daglish-NSAG-Sanctions.pdf> accessed 2 June 2024.

50 ICRC, 'International Criminal Court' (*International Committee of the Red Cross,* 29 October 2010) <https://www.icrc.org/en/document/international-criminal-court> accessed 2 June 2024.

51 See Sharon Weill, 'Building Respect for IHL Through National Courts' (2014) 96(895/896) International Review of the Red Cross 859.

52 Jakob Kellenberger, 'The Role of the International Committee of the Red Cross' in Andrew Clapham and Paola Gaeta (eds), *The Oxford Handbook of International Law in Armed Conflict* (Oxford University Press 2014) 20-34.

53 Sivakumaran (n 6) 145.

54 Christoph Koettl, 'Sensors Everywhere: Using Satellites and Mobile Phones to Reduce Information Uncertainty in Human Rights Crisis Research' (2017) 11 Genocide Studies and Prevention 36.

55 See, for example, Lara Hakki, Eric Stover and Rohini J. Haar, 'Breaking the Silence: Advocacy and Accountability for Attacks on

Hospitals in Armed Conflict' (2020) 102(915) International Review of the Red Cross 1201.

56 See Matthew Happold, 'The Conference of High Contracting Parties to the Fourth Geneva Convention' (2001) 4 Yearbook of International Humanitarian Law 389; ICRC, *Conference of High Contracting Parties to the Fourth Geneva Convention: Statement by the International Committee of the Red Cross, Geneva, 5 December 2001* (International Committee of the Red Cross 15 December 2001).